Your life. Your choice.

"A useful and thoughtful book, explaining how, with help, it is possible to reduce many risks of disease. This is a comprehensive guide in primary preventative health care and an important read for those of the general public, wanting to optimise their health. Useful for any in the medical profession, so they may better understand what their patients are talking about."

Dr KRH Adams FRCP. BA. Retired
Specialist in Geriatric Medicine.
Consultant in Rheumatology and
Founder & Clinical Director
of the Pain Clinic.

"The Government is committed, not only to providing an NHS that is able to meet the demands, but to encouraging the general public in practices that will prevent disease and promote good health ... and sends his best wishes for the book's success."

Letter from the office of
Health Secretary, Matt Hancock:

"I was enlightened by the book and am amazed that with the knowledge and technology of today we are still using so many chemicals in our food and our household products which is affecting our health and shortening our lives. An understanding on how to rise above any difficulties as set out in Part 10 is a valuable addition to this book."

Sheila J Collins. Retired SRN SCM.
Was also registered in the USA.

"As a GP I found this book quite thought provoking particularly about people taking personal responsibility for keeping fit and as active as possible while also recognising the environmental and lifestyle issues that we need to be aware of in support of our immune system. I found the rundown of alternative therapies that are now available, and how they can support our health, also very interesting."

Dr Stevan Johl B.Med.Sci,
MBChB, MRCGP

"As a member of the public I found this book contains much useful information on how we can take an active part to prevent disease. I was also very interested to learn about The Secret to achieve whatever goals and dreams we have, whether financial or otherwise. A positive route in reducing stress, one of the main reasons for the cause of disease."

Sara Molinari . A Retired
Professional Entertainer.

Your Life.
Your Choice.

For Health and Success in the 21st Century

Gretchen Pyves MSc.
Retired: SRN. SCM.
HV Cert.

Copyright © Gretchen Pyves 2018
Published by MG Publications

All rights reserved
Unauthorised duplication contravenes existing laws

British Library Cataloguing-in-Publication data
A catalogue record for this book is available from the British Library

ISBN: 978-1-5272-3115-3
Printed and bound by Severn, Gloucester

Contents

Preface	3
Part 1: Introduction	7
Beveridge Report	7
Part 2: Our Immune system	13
Stress	14
Infection	15
Pollutants	16
Chemicals	16
Antibiotics	17
Over the counter chemicals	19
Skin Care/Cosmetics	20
Aluminium	21
Fluoride	22
Care of Teeth	23
Household Cleaners	23
Electromagnetic Fields	25
Cell Phones	26
Microwave ovens	26
Part 3: Foods	29
Fast Foods	30
Trans Fats	32

Saturated Fats	33
Soy Milk	34
Sweeteners	34
Fruit Drinks	35
Conclusion	36
Part 4: Addictions	**39**
Smoking	39
Vaping	41
Alcohol	41
Illegal Drugs	42
Compulsive Buying Disorder	43
Mobile Phones	44
Gambling	44
Part 5: Ways to maintain Health	**47**
Water	47
Himalyan Rock salt	50
Organic Food	51
Food Supplements	51
Exercise	53
Cycling	54
Dancing	54
Swimming	54
Team Sports	55
Walking/Gym	55
Part 6: Our mind can heal us	**57**
The Healing Code	58

Meditation	59
Music	60
EFT	61
Mind Management (Chimp paradox)	62
Part 7: Home Supporting Methods	**65**
Air Ionisers	65
Salt Lamps	66
Infrared Saunas	67
Hair Tissue Mineral Analysis	68
Airnergy	68
Polaraid Health Disc	69
Pulsed Electromagnetic Fields	69
Resperate	70
Scenar	70
Zona Plus	72
Ways to minimise Harmful radiation Sources	**73**
Earthing	73
Geopathic Stress	74
WiFi	74
Q-Link	75
Blushield	76
Earthcalm	76
Part 8: Classes Promoting Health with qualified Practitioners	**79**
Tai Qi	79
Yoga	80

Pilates	81
Part 9: Health Maintenance with trained Practitioners	85
Acupuncture	85
Acupressure	86
Alexander Technique	86
Ayurvedic Medicine	87
Bioenergetics	88
Bioresonance/MORA Therapy	88
Bowen Technique	90
Chelation Therapy	92
Chiropractic & Osteopathy	94
Epigenetics	95
Homeopathy	97
Kinesiology	98
Massage	98
Reflexology	99
Reiki	99
Rolfing	100
The Zenni Method	101
Part 10: Wealth & Success – We have a choice	103
Steps to achieve Wealth & Success	106
Financial Education	109
Summary	119
Notes and References	122
About the Author	137

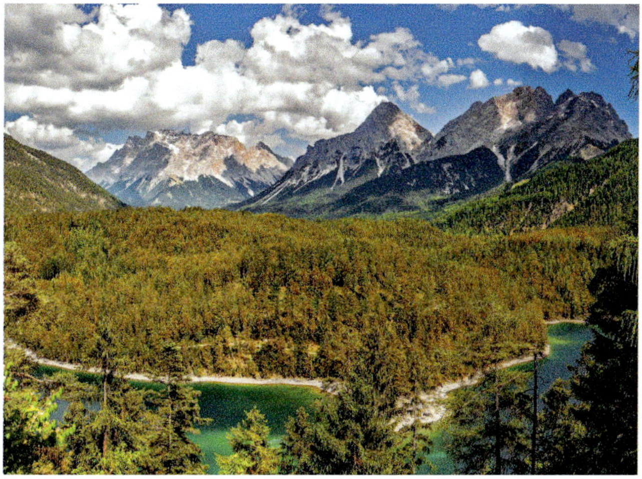

A wise man should consider
that health is the greatest of human blessings,
and learn how by his own thought
to derive benefit from his illnesses

                              Hippocrates

Preface

Hello dear reader,

Have you ever wondered why we get ill and develop diseases?

Have you ever wondered why some people are more successful or wealthier than others?

These two important life components are the subject of this book. They are, after all, our means to happiness and well-being.

I trained as a General Nurse at Guy's Hospital London. My interest has always been in health matters and especially why diseases occur in the first place, in other words why? – What is the cause? Over the years, this interest has grown to seek ways to avoid, as far as is possible, those damaging effects we are all exposed to from the environment we live in and which can lead on to disease. I have brought together many of these, so that you too will have this knowledge and thus be able to make decisions as to your own way of life.

Health management books abound on how to cure this or heal that. What is not so available are the many ways that we are open to damage. There is a mountain of knowledge out there, going back to very early times and ancient wisdom, which still holds true but also includes present day developments. We have the means to prevent disease, to a great extent and live out our life in happiness and contentment. This knowledge begins the journey. By following these well-trodden and researched paths, I have gathered together, we can, to a greater extent determine our own health.

Our life path is made up of the choices we make. In order to make sound choices we need to have as much information as possible on which to base those choices.

We now know that every person has an absolutely miraculous healing system in their body that can heal any physical or non-physical issue that a person might have and these ways are included. It is after all our responsibility in the way we live, to avoid and prevent illness and disease. You will have a great deal to choose from. Focussing on perfect health is something we can all do within and for ourselves, despite what may be happening all around us.

Please note this book is in no way prescriptive regarding health and therefore does not deal, as such, with ways to heal or cure disease. It is to do with setting out proven ways to prevent ill health as far as is possible. In other words it is about damage limitation and aiding our bodies to maintain health. It is not a substitute for consulting with your medical practitioner on your own medical problems. The two are not mutually exclusive.

It is also known that we determine our life path and that our current life is as a result of past thoughts. I touch on the wisdom passed down through the ages by successful men and women who have applied this knowledge to acquire massive wealth and how some have overcome obstacles and achieved what many would regard as impossible. You now have access to this and can benefit from this knowledge. By knowing and understanding the power you have, you can set out the Life of your Choice. Enjoy the journey you have before you to determine your path in life and accomplish whatever you so desire.

People act on what they believe in, and so all the things we do, are based on what we know at any one time, because of these beliefs. Finding more about any given subject can cause us to rethink and maybe alter our beliefs.

"Whatever your mind can conceive and believe the mind can achieve"
—Napolean Hill[1]

With my love and may you find continual happiness and peace in your life.

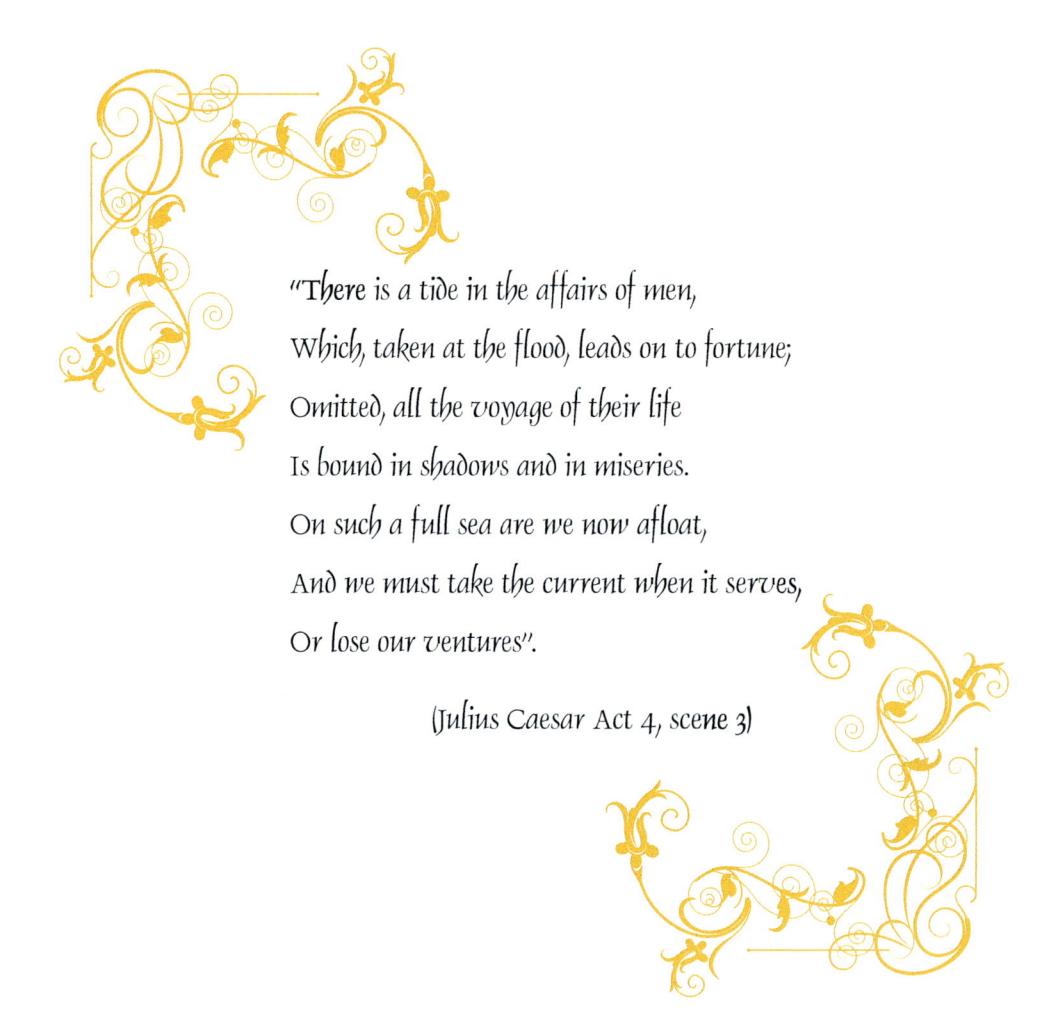

"There is a tide in the affairs of men,
Which, taken at the flood, leads on to fortune;
Omitted, all the voyage of their life
Is bound in shadows and in miseries.
On such a full sea are we now afloat,
And we must take the current when it serves,
Or lose our ventures".

(Julius Caesar Act 4, scene 3)

Part 1: Introduction

As I write this in early 2018, our National Health Service is apparently in chaos, being swamped by the sheer numbers of people requiring medical attention.

More and more people perceive their need for medical help and the system appears to be collapsing under the strain. We are now, to put it bluntly, an ill health society. The system is becoming overloaded to a point of serious concern. Is there another way?

The solution, seen by those in the Health Service, is to ask for more money to fund more doctors, more nurses and more hospitals and more home care to deal with this ever increasing perceived need. In order to understand this better I am firstly going to take a look at the birth of our Health Service and the ethos on which it was based, because it seems to me, that this has been a contributory factor in this avalanche of ill health.

The Beveridge Report[2]

In 1941 the then Labour Government headed by Aneurin Bevan appointed Sir William Beveridge to report on the Social Insurances & Allied Services to solve the problems of Want, Disease, Squalor and Idleness. Beveridge became a leading authority on unemployment and social security known now as the Welfare State.

Beveridge, did not however, intend that Britain should become a nanny state. On the contrary he fully believed that individuals should always seek to improve their lot by hard work and thrift, but also that they needed help along the way. So in 1948, a state funded health care

Photo above: Hippocrates

system was established, and the process of setting up the National Health Service with free medical treatment for all, began. This, together with the social security system, established that the population of the UK would be protected 'from the cradle to the grave'.

This Bill was hailed as the great achievement of the Labour Government.

So where are we now, particularly in terms of our Health Service? At this point it is useful to remind ourselves of Hippocrates and his wisdom as the founder of medicine. Hippocrates was born around 460 BC on the island of Kos, Greece.

He was regarded as the greatest physician of his time and he based his medical practice on his observations and study of the human body. He held the belief that illness had a physical and a rational explanation. Hippocrates believed that the body must be treated as a whole and not just as a series of parts.

Over the years the general population has come to expect and even demand that the doctor prescribes a pill for their ailments, in the belief that a pill will solve their problem without any other changes to their lifestyle. Certainly, when the pioneers of pharmaceutical drugs produced antibiotics, they were hailed as life savers and so it was for those patients who were responsive and became well. At that time bacteria were treated, as they were not, as yet, resistant to antibiotics. Vaccines were also being developed for poliomyelitis and later on for diphtheria, smallpox and certain forms of meningitis. This resulted in many incidences of the diseases of that period, being reduced or treated satisfactorily. The pharmaceutical industry was hailed as a great boon in treating them. However, over the years since then, pharmaceutical companies have strived to find more and more ways to deal with many conditions affecting all parts of our bodies with their chemical products.

Doctors are in large part prescribing drugs because the pharmaceutical companys purport to provide medicines which can cure. In addition patients believe that this is how to be cured and are demanding them. It is now well known that bacteria are becoming resistant to many drugs in use and the pharmaceutical industry is constantly developing new drugs to attempt to deal with ailments. Doctors rarely have the time, to find out what is going on in a person's life in terms of their lifestyle, or even to be able to give advice on matters such as healthy eating. Furthermore doctors are not sufficiently trained in nutrition. A change needs to come, both from the public and the doctors, to understand and follow ways to stay healthy. Kings Fund 2010[3].

In the western world we are in fact causing our own deaths, since 80% of diseases are caused by poor diet and lifestyle choices. WDDTY Dec 2017[4].

In addition over the counter medicines, which are readily available without a prescription, all contain chemicals which can adversely affect our organs and in the long run will lead to illness and diseases through the damage they cause.

This is a serious state of affairs. Chronic illnesses are on the increase as our healthcare system has no provision for taking a proactive role to promote healthy living and with nowhere else to go, people turn first and foremost to the doctor to 'fix' their ailments with a pill, with no thought as to why the problem has arisen in the first place.

Putting money into finding more chemical cures to deal with diseases of the heart, diabetes and cancer, to name a few, are in fact the creation of this demand, as people see this as the answer, by having no other legitimate way presented to them. Until it is recognised that both the individual and the health system need to take a proactive role in maintaining healthy lifestyles through healthy food intake, sufficient exercise together with the avoidance of toxic substances, we will continue on the downward spiral of ill health. Is it any wonder that some people are beginning to feel they want to gain some measure of power over their health and to seek appropriate means to do so?

If you are one of those who are getting fed up with the medical industry that treats every problem by throwing prescriptions at it, then I trust this book will be of some help.

The question now is "What can we do to look after the health of our bodies and take good care for ourselves?" My main focus has been to identify and show how, and by what means, we can take this responsibility, in order to go a long way in preventing disease.

It could be argued that our NHS is also there for the prevention of disease. Let us consider this and the ways this is undertaken:
Immunisation programmes together with mass of screening procedures to identify whether disease is present e.g. mammograms, cervical smears,

a variety of blood tests, X-Rays and ultrasound to name a few. When disease is found through these procedures, there is every likelihood that drugs will be prescribed or surgical procedures carried out, all with the aim to prevent further damage.

The focus for the NHS is all about preventing further development of identified illnesses/diseases. This type of clinical prevention is known as secondary prevention, in other words identifying whether an illnesses is present and then preventing it's advancement by clinical treatment or surgery.

This book is different; it is all about the many causes of disease, why we get ill in the first place. This is primary prevention.

Our health is under siege from every direction. There are a vast number of threats which surround us. Understanding and knowing what these are and more importantly, how to avoid them, allows us to make informed decisions on how we manage our lives.

Disease is largely the result of the environment to which we have been exposed, so logically it is the environmental issues that we firstly need to address. I have gathered together as comprehensive a list, as has been possible, showing the many ways in which we are exposed to this plethora of damage.

Then, in order to sustain and support our own health, I have presented some researched and trusted ways that are available, to help us. These include well-known conventional practices, universally believed to be 'safe' and which can have a positive impact on maintaining and improving our health. With this knowledge, you can draw your own conclusions as to whether you wish to embrace them with greater understanding of the health benefits to you and your family.

However these should not be considered replacements for professional medical treatment, and it remains the responsibility of the reader to decide when to seek medical advice where they perceive their symptoms require a diagnosis.

We need to remember that we are natural beings. We are children of the Universe. We are of nature in the same way as the plants and the animals. Let us embrace this concept and enjoy our life. We are the sole caretakers of our wonderful bodies and we also need to follow the Hippocratic Oath to "First do no harm".

Over the centuries, the Hippocratic oath has been rewritten often in order to suit the values of different cultures influenced by Greek medicine. Contrary to popular belief, the Hippocratic Oath is not required by most modern medical schools, although some have adopted modern versions that suit many in the profession in the 21st century. It also does not explicitly contain the phrase, "First, do no harm," which is commonly attributed to it.

Finally, a book such as this, needs to consider human beings holistically i.e. Body Mind and Spirit, so all of these have been included. Each of these parts cannot function without the others also being addressed, as they are without question, all part of our makeup and affect each other. When one area is distressed or ignored then there are repercussions throughout the whole body system.

One of the many causes of stress is poverty. I have always been interested to observe that there are some very successful people, who seem to rise above their roots, both financially and socially despite (or perhaps because of) very poor backgrounds. Many books have been written on this and the reference section allows you access to these. I have drawn on the wisdom of these authors to introduce you to the paths they have trodden in achieving their goals. What is quite clear is that they have followed a definite Code, which has specific 'rules'. They all knew and understood this 'secret' to wealth and success.

Wealth has many meanings. If we only focus on financial wealth we need to remind ourselves, that wealth alone will not bring either health or happiness. It will, however, help towards achieving a better lifestyle with less financial stress.

I trust you will enjoy reading all parts of this book and take from it what seems right for you.

Natural forces within us are
the true healers of disease.

                                        Hippocrates

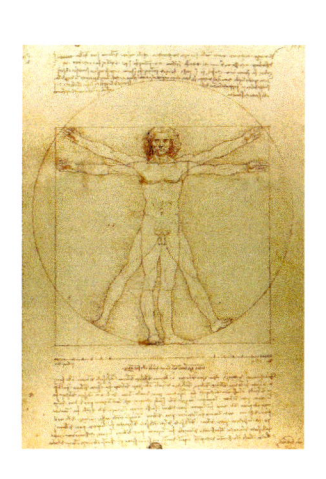

Part 2: Our Immune System

Success in overcoming every health issue you're concerned about – from the common cold to serious diseases such as cancer, diabetes, heart disease, prostate, fibromyalgia, rheumatoid arthritis, allergies, asthma, HIV/AIDS, hepatitis, tuberculosis, or chronic fatigue syndrome – is dependent on how secure your immune system is.

Our immune system is our body's defence against infection and illness. It recognises the cells that make up our body, and will try to get rid of anything unfamiliar. It will destroy germs (bacteria and viruses) and parasites. We are host to a great army of micro-organisms and different types of white blood cells fighting on our behalf, giving us vital protection against diseases. In good health we make about 1000 million of them every day in our bone marrow. Some of these cells, called macrophages, constantly patrol our body, destroying germs as soon as they enter.

This is our 'natural' or inborn immunity. If an infection begins to take hold, our body fights back with an even more powerful defences in the form of white T and B blood cells, called lymphocytes. They give acquired immunity, so that the same germ can never make us as ill again. A weakened immune system can lead to colds, flu and disease and is often the result of a poor diet, stress and the unhealthy ways in which we live.

Our immune system is at work constantly, protecting us against bacteria and diseases and it is logical that it can only deal with so much. If it is being compromised over and over again, it is not hard to understand that it will be less than efficient. Health needs to be looked

Photo above: Leonardo da Vinci – Vitruvian Man

at as a systemic state. In other words the body will react at any time, to whatever is creating any kind of stress, and it will then attempt to repair.

Anything that weakens this immune system can lead to a secondary immunodeficiency disorder resulting in vulnerability to a host of diseases and illnesses. Our immune system is capable of healing any issue with amazing speed and efficiency. Healing only ever happens if our immune system is strong. This is our Code to Health.

While we cannot predict when we will leave this earth, or for what reason, we can at least ensure that we live our lives to the best of our ability while we are here. The health of our bodies is our responsibility and ours alone and our health is enhanced by making sound and informed choices. We are the caretakers of our wonderful bodies. When we have sufficient knowledge we can make our own informed choices as to our lifestyle and be able take a pro-active role in looking after our very own in-built health system.

As human beings, like all living things, we have an exquisite capacity to selfheal. What is needed is the right environment for that to happen. Choosing a lifestyle that will support our immune system is the key to maintaining our health. In other words, "Living wisely in accordance with natural laws" Selye[5].

The question then arises; if we already have this in-built way to maintain health, how is it we succumb to any illness/disease? My one purpose in the following pages is to show how and why some lifestyle practices can lead to illness and disease. Decisions can only be taken with the information we have.

Let us now examine the many ways we compromise our Immune System.

Stress

It is true to say that stress is the cause of all illness and disease. Cortisol is vital for life, however when stress occurs this triggers an overload of this chemical which can damage our brains and weaken our cardiovascular and immune systems over time. The first things stress turns off are the healing and immune systems. However when these are turned back on they are capable of healing just about anything.

Stress can result from physical, chemical or emotional triggers. It matters little which type of stress is experienced, the body will react in the same way to a greater or lesser degree, depending on the level being experienced.

If stressful conditions persist the body will continue to adapt in order to maintain homeostasis and it does so by continually flooding the body with cortisol. This results in an increased heart rate, a rise in blood pressure, a rise in blood sugar levels and a rise in LDL Cholesterol (bad cholesterol). At the same time the blood to our gut will diminish, creating stomach and digestive problems. These are all very natural reactions but if experienced over a sustained period of time they will inevitably lead to our immune system being compromised. The primary job of our immune system is to maintain both a level of homeostasis and the regeneration of cells so that we enjoy optimum health. It is the process by which all organs of our body rely on, to survive.

The release of these stress hormones also causes hyper oxidation leading to the formation of free radicals which are one of the basic and damaging processes in the body, at the cellular and tissue level. Stress in its continued form affects the adrenal glands which are situated at the top of each kidney. These are the glands that produce cortisol which is essential for life. However with prolonged stress they become exhausted by their continual production of cortisol in attempting to regain homeostasis. This will eventually lead to adrenal failure. A stressful lifestyle, of whatever nature creates problems throughout the body and for its coping mechanism. Over time illness and disease will develop.

Infection

Infectious diseases have made a powerful comeback since the late 1970s. The single most threatening aspect of this has been the appearance of new strains of disease-causing bacteria that have become resistant to antibiotics. These bacteria have developed sophisticated mechanisms of resistance against almost every antibiotic invented thus far. According to one respected infectious disease researcher, Dr Alexander Tomasz[6], these resistant bacteria mutate from one type to another. They can travel over large distances, creating high incidences of infection. These bacteria are resistant to all chemical agents in the current medical arsenal and pose an ever-increasing problem.

I now set out yet further ways our immune system is compromised, with an explanation as to what damage can occur as a consequence.

Pollutants

Professor Dame Sally Davies[7], England's Chief Medical Officer, in her annual report March 2018, stated that there is growing evidence that pollution, notably air pollution, increases risk of infectious disease.

We all know the environmental impacts of pollution – but what is less recognised is the impact on health.

Dame Sally said many pollutants are risk factors for diseases such as cardiovascular disease, cancer and asthma.

Her report also calls for Public Health England to support local authorities by compiling available, up-to-date evidence on the health impacts of pollution.

Addressing pollution is therefore all about disease prevention.

Chemicals

Unquestionably, many of the chemical sources with which we now have contact, have been in existence for centuries. However, today we are exposed to a greater variety of chemicals, with increased concentration, than was the case for our ancestors.

Although the human body is known to be very accommodating, ecological alterations are now occurring at a faster rate than our bodies are able to adapt. We are now faced with a situation where inadequacies or uncertainties around the manufacture, use, storage, and disposal of toxic chemicals, have resulted in an overwhelming number of environmentally induced illnesses.

Since 1965, over 4 million distinct chemical compounds have been reported in scientific literature. Over 6000 new chemicals were added to this list between 1965 and 1978. As of 1981, of over 70,000 chemicals in commercial production, 3,000 have been identified as intentionally added to our food supplies and over 700 to our drinking water. During food processing and storage a further 10,000 other compounds can become an integral part of many commonly used foods. Added to this list of potential body toxins, petrochemicals, industrial waste, medical and street drugs, and radiation from X-rays, nuclear fallout and flying together with tons of pesticides, herbicides, and insecticides, the result is an incredible chemical avalanche which has engulfed the human race in a relatively short period of evolutionary history.

There is currently a wealth of scientific evidence showing that thousands of drugs, preservatives, pesticides, and other pollutants remain stored in the body long after exposure. We now know, for example, that the storage of a chlorinated pesticide, such as the metabolites of DDT, has a half-life of between 20 and 50 years in the fat deposits of humans. According to the U.S. Environmental Protection Agency over 400 chemicals have been detected in human tissue; 48 were found in adipose tissue, 40 in breastmilk, 73 in the liver and over 250 in the blood.

The process of bodily accumulation and storage of toxins is known as "toxic bio-accumulation". Although the predominant storage site in the body is the fatty tissue, toxins may re-enter the bloodstream during times of physical stress (e.g. illness, fasting, excessive heat, exercise) or emotional stress. Every organ, that is accessible to these chemicals, which has been mobilized or released from the fat, is being continually exposed at low levels. As stated by Dr William L. Marcus[8], Senior Advisor and Chief Toxicologist for the U.S. Environmental Protection Agency, "It's a chronic exposure. That's why chemicals like dioxin, even in small amounts, are extremely dangerous. Unfortunately the human body has no previous experience with these chemicals and there is no natural machinery in the body to break them down, much less eliminate them".

Antibiotics

One of the most frequent prescriptions doctors issue to their patients, is for antibiotics. It is now well accepted that the overuse of antibiotics has effectively brought about resistance in the invading bacteria.

Although antibiotics are still very important to counter infection and disease in the process of destroying the specific invading bacteria, they also destroy much of the good bacteria in our gut which form the first line of defence. Their name gives the clue as to how they perform – anti-biotic so they can destroy our good gut bacteria as well. Long time and frequent intake of antibiotics will lead to our gut being unable to deal with harmful bacteria which then multiply and start to leak through our gut into our circulatory system.

As increased amounts of bad bacteria in our gut leaks out into our blood stream they cause a host of inflammatory problems creating general ill health, and manifesting in a whole host of disorders. Dr Keith Scott-Mumby[9] has written about the great need to maintain a healthy gut in order to prevent the bad bacteria from flourishing and causing damage throughout the body. There is a fine balance in using antibiotics and Doctors are themselves, now understanding that they are no longer the panacea to achieve health.

We can no longer turn a blind eye to the side effects of the drugs that are being given. There is also nothing "side" about the effects; they are unwanted direct effects of the drugs. Are there other ways? (see Colloidal Silver: British Medical Journal 1932[10]).

It is a sign of our times that patients expect and in fact can demand that their Doctor prescribes a drug to deal with their problems. "A pill to cure without due regard for the lifestyle of their patient". Time constraints prevent Doctors from spending time with their patients to ascertain what could be some of the causal factors in their life. Lifestyle is Key.

The question needs to be asked, as to why Doctors are not given any real training in nutrition – a vital component of our wellbeing. This surely seems deeply unwise since "we are what we eat and absorb". Doctors have no other means at their disposal, except to treat their patients with chemicals – together with their damaging side effects. It is their main 'go to' in the arsenal of treatments available. Big pharma has a great deal of influence over what our GP's use in their practice.

New thinking is beginning to emerge in respect of the future of medicine and according to William Tiller[11], Nobel Prize Laureate, this will be focused on controlling energy in the body. This is supported by George Crile[12]. MD. Founder of the Cleveland Clinic (1864–1943) who, states that "In the future diseases are to be diagnosed and prevented via energy field assessment". Although such thinking is new to the west it has been practiced by the Chinese for many years and is the basis of many alternative practices including acupuncture. Furthermore Albert Einstein[13] demonstrated that everything comes down to energy. This will be explored further when on the subject of stress.

A group of 21 doctors in California led by Bolazs Bodai[14] Director of the Breast Cancer Survivorship Institute in Sacramento California, are calling for a complete overhaul of the current medical system which treats disease with drugs or surgery without looking deeper into the lifestyle causes. They are challenging the pharmaceutical industry's practises and their hold over doctors, which can be seen as a declaration of independence from big pharma. They are suggesting that Lifestyle Medical Centres need to be set up inside established health care buildings, to provide additional health and supportive services, other than those offered by the current system. WDDTY Dec 2017[14]. People will have a choice.

Aside from the drugs we are prescribed, there are a host of other chemical substances, mainly developed by pharmaceutical companies. I now present some of these.

Over the counter chemicals

Chemists offer an array of chemical 'cures', for all manner of ailments from the common cold and chesty coughs to pain of all kinds and these chemicals are obtainable over the counter, without a prescription.

When suffering from pain it an easy option to consume over-the-counter painkillers such as ibuprofen, aspirin and paracetamol. It is now known that painkilling drugs also affect that part of the brain that influences social awareness. This can result in the numbing our feelings towards others. In cases of severe pain and the increased intake of these drugs, the body can readily crave and become addicted to them. Painkillers are among the most frequently bought over the counter drugs without a prescription. In Britain people take an average of 373 painkillers every year. WDDTY May 2108[15]. The judgements people make while on these drugs, could well be affected in view of this. This lack of social awareness in society, now being created by the use of these drugs, is surely a matter of some concern. A question occurs as to whether this is manifesting itself in an increasing crime rate.

An examination of the contents of prescriptions or any over-the-counter medicine will reveal a host of chemicals which are certainly not natural. This is an added strain on our immune system which has to eliminate these chemicals to offset the damage they can cause, but they are brushed aside and labelled 'side effects'! Fortunately products now have to be clearly labelled so we can at least decide whether we want to impose these 'side effects' on our bodies, because not only has our immune system to deal with the original problem, for which the chemical was prescribed, it also has to deal with the additional damaging effects these chemicals can cause. Some are more difficult than others to eliminate and the chemical damage to our bodies can take its toll. The pharmaceutical industry is big business and claims to cure a variety of diseases. However, we need to ask ourselves, if this is such a marvellous way, how come the population is not fighting fit? It is in fact just the opposite.

The notion that there is a chemical pill or potion to alleviate or cure any illness is one that to a large extent has been put out by the pharmaceutical companies who both test and promote them. Doctors anxious to give 'effective' treatments rely on these drugs. The general public believes the doctor knows best. Few understand the damage that these chemicals can cause, and they swallow them unaware. Education and greater understanding will hopefully lead to a healthier attitude. The rationale for pharmaceutical medicines rests on the premise that chemical processes in the body progress in a linear and orderly fashion. We now know that chemical reactions in the body are distinctly not linear but chaotic, thus undermining such rationale. WDDTY May 2015[16].

Skin Care/Cosmetics

Our skin is the largest organ of our body and since it is porous, it absorbs whatever we put on it. Exposure from any source, whether occupational, cosmetic, or pharmaceutical, means that it enters our body. When it comes to living a healthy and natural lifestyle, what you put on your body is just as significant as what you put in your body. It is therefore important to pay close attention to the ingredients in our skin care products. The cosmetics industry is big business. We apply lotions and potions to our skin with the intention of improving our looks but many body care products contain a cocktail of carcinogenic chemicals, allergens, and irritants. These all have to be eliminated by the immune system, thus creating an extra job for it to accomplish and causing further stress.

By selecting natural and non-chemical products for yourself and your family, in soap, toothpaste, deodorants, shampoo, moisturisers and suntan lotion, you will be taking a big step towards maintaining a healthier lifestyle and not compromising your immune system. The developing organs of babies and children are particularly sensitive to chemicals so it is really important to use natural products while pregnant and later for your youngsters. These are all available at reputable health stores and on line.

Using these will lower the effects of potentially damaging chemicals such as Sodium Lauryl Sulphate commonly known as SLS, which is a widely used and inexpensive chemical found in many mainstream personal hygiene products such as shampoos, toothpastes, mouthwashes, bodywash, soaps, detergents and body and various cleaning products. A study published in the Journal of the American College of Toxicology[17] found sodium lauryl sulphate and ammonium lauryl sulphate to be irritants, so definitely not healthy ingredients to lather onto the body's largest organ, the skin.

Other products containing SLS include; pesticides, industrial cleaning products, floor cleaners, engine degreasers and carwash soaps. It must be noted that these particular cleaning products use a concentrated form of the chemical.

Other studies state that SLS is not dangerous for human use - Environmental Health Insights[18] as according to them, SLS is only a "moderate hazard" that has been wrongly linked to cancer, neurotoxicity, organ toxicity, skin irritation and endocrine disruption.

Individuals should make their own choices about the health risks that they are willing to take when using any product, in order to prevent an overload of stress to their immune system.

Aluminium

Studies, in recent years, have theorized that aluminium-based antiperspirants may increase the risk for breast cancer. According to the authors of these studies, most breast cancers develop in the upper outer part of the breast – the area closest to the armpit, which is where antiperspirants are applied.

Deodorants contain aluminium and synthetic fragrances. These are undesirable components many people are sensitive to. If you find that your underarms are irritated, it may be an allergic reaction to the aluminium, which is toxic to the body: Drs Daniel Krewski et al[19].

High levels of aluminium in the body have also been shown to have neurotoxic effects on bone and possibly reproduction. This occurs when the amount of aluminium consumed exceeds the body's capacity to excrete it, because the aluminium along with mercury from amalgam fillings is then deposited in our bodies and can damage the brain. Aluminium has been associated with a variety of health issues, including: breast cancer, Alzheimer's disease, bone disorders and kidney problems. See also Dr Edward Group[20].

While some studies have indicated abnormal volumes of aluminium in the brain tissue of Alzheimer patients, other studies show no correlation between aluminium intake and Alzheimer's. These theories have caused a lot of discussions, as there are many different opinions. As in all products we use, each one of us has to make up their own mind on the evidence available.

Fluoride

A word here about fluoride, as it is claimed by a great many professionals to have beneficial effects on the teeth and gums.

The NHS is clear that "Brushing your teeth thoroughly with fluoride toothpaste is one of the most effective ways of preventing tooth decay". It is said to help reduce dental caries as it is then swallowed.

However according to Dr Edward Group[21] "Fluoride is one of the most toxic substances known to man, yet its inclusion is in virtually every brand of toothpaste". In addition Dr Dean Burke's[22] view supports this by stating "fluoride causes more human cancer deaths and causes it faster than any other chemical".

Dr Mercola's[23] site states that: 'According to a 500-page scientific review, fluoride is an endocrine disruptor that can affect your bones, brain, thyroid gland, pineal gland and even your blood sugar levels'.

There have been over 34 human studies and 100 animal studies linking fluoride to brain damage, including lower IQ in children, and these studies have shown that fluoride toxicity can lead to a wide variety of health problems. Further, the fluoride added to most water supplies is not the naturally occurring variety but rather fluorosilicic acid. This captured fluoride acid is the most contaminated chemical added to public water supplies. Possible risks include cancer due to the acid's elevated arsenic content, as well as neurotoxic consequences. Mercola[23].

A study in the Lancet in 2014[24] on the use of fluoride and neurodevelopmental toxicity, states there are still more questions than answers.

These are widely held differing views. We need to decide for ourselves the route to take.

Care of the teeth

There is a very good reason why you need to clean your teeth at least twice a day and floss before going to bed. Our saliva does help to wash away the food we have eaten and remove the bacteria developing from food particles lodged between our teeth, during the day, but at night that flow is reduced and if not removed, these food particles will putrefy. The gums will then become infected and this infection will find its way into the blood stream, creating inflammation within the arteries. So to avoid bacteria multiplying in your mouth in the first place, keep your teeth free from any food debris. This is an important twice or more daily task that will go a long way to helping our immune system as well as protecting our teeth.

Surely this is an easy practice to help keep our bodies free, at least from one source of bacteria causing inflammation which, as we know, leads to heart disease and the development of other problems like arteriosclerosis and high blood pressure. Women, who suffer from periodontal disease, whereby the gums become infected by dental plaque, are more likely to suffer from breast cancer. (WDDTY Feb 2016[25]). It is also advisable to leave at least a half hour after eating, before brushing the teeth, to enable the acid in the mouth to reduce, thus saving the tooth enamel from damage. In addition the average toothbrush harbours millions of pathogens, so it is advisable to rinse your toothbrush in boiling water every 3 days.

Household Cleaners

When we buy commercial cleaning products, we expect them to do one thing: clean! We use a wide array of scents, soaps, detergents, bleaching agents, softeners, scourers, polishes, and specialized cleaners for bathrooms, glass, drains, and ovens to keep our homes sparkling and sweet-smelling. But while the chemicals in these cleaners will foam, bleach, and disinfect to make our dishes, bathtubs and countertops gleaming and germ-free, many also contribute to indoor air pollution, are poisonous if ingested and can be harmful if inhaled or touched. In fact, some cleaners are among the most toxic products found in the home e.g. bleach.

Cleaning ingredients vary in terms of the type of health hazard they pose. Some cause acute, or immediate, hazards such as skin or respiratory irritation, watery eyes, or chemical burns, while others are associated with chronic and possible long-term effects on their lungs.

The most acutely hazardous cleaning products are corrosive drain cleaners, oven cleaners, and acidic toilet bowl cleaners, according to Philip Dickey[26] of the Washington Toxics Coalition. Corrosive chemicals can cause severe burns on eyes, skin and if ingested, on the throat and oesophagus. Ingredients with high acute toxicity include chlorine bleach and ammonia, which produce fumes that are highly irritating to eyes, nose, throat and lungs, and should not be used by people with asthma or lung or heart problems. These two chemicals pose an added threat in that they can react with each other or other chemicals to form lung-damaging gases. Combining products that contain chlorine and ammonia or ammonia and lye (in some oven cleaners) produces chloramine gas, while chlorine combined with acids (commonly used in toilet bowl cleaners) forms toxic chlorine gas.

Fragrances added to many cleaners, most notably laundry detergents and fabric softeners, may cause acute reactions such as respiratory irritation, headache, sneezing, and watery eyes in sensitive individuals or are allergic for asthma sufferers. The National Institute of Occupational Safety and Health[27] has found that one-third of the substances used in the fragrance industry are toxic. But because the chemical formulas of fragrances are considered trade secrets, companies are not required to list their ingredients but merely label them as containing "fragrance." Other ingredients in cleaners may have low to acute toxicity but contribute to long-term health problems, such as cancer or hormone disruption.

Washing detergents and can cause the growth of drug-resistant bacteria. Air fresheners contain secret fragrance mixtures and chemicals that can trigger allergies and asthma.

One way to avoid these damaging chemicals is to use natural products made from simple ingredients like white vinegar, washing soda, and baking soda, which don't have the damaging effects of the harmful chemicals used in most products. This will allow the immune system to function without the added burden of having to eliminate them.

Electro Magnetic Fields

> *"The greatest polluting element in the earth's environment is the proliferation of electromagnetic fields."*
> —Dr Robert Becker[28]

Where do Electromagnetic Fields Come From? Simply put, EMFs come from electricity: in your home: DECT cordless phones, hairdryers, vacuums, refrigerators, microwave ovens, irons, televisions Wi-Fi, etc. in your office: computers, fluorescent or halogen lighting, fax machines, photocopiers, scanners and cell phones. Outside: power lines (high voltage cables either overhead or buried in the ground), transformers (the grey cylinders raised up on poles that look like trash cans), electricity substations, cell phone towers, cities that provide city-wide wireless internet (Wi-Fi) and electromagnetic radiation from near neighbours' electronic equipment. They are areas of energy that surround all electronic devices.

Dr Pawluk[29] explains that our bodies themselves are electromagnetic. The body's own internal magnetic fields are generated by the extraordinary amount of internal electrical activity that keeps our bodies alive. This produces complex electrical activity in several different types of cells, including neurons, endocrine, and muscle cells — all called "excitable cells". This creates our own magnetic field which then interacts with all of the other magnetic fields on the planet and controls our basic chemistry.

The earth has its own natural electromagnetic field, which as humans, we are beneficially in tune with. However where there are underground streams, sewers, water pipes, electricity, tunnels and underground railways, mineral formations and geological faults running beneath our properties, these can distort these natural electromagnetic fields, creating Geopathic Stress. For practical purposes, people are likely to be affected if their home, office, etc. is located at any height at all above these harmful rays, and is often referred to as 'sick building syndrome'. As this compromises our immune system, it will over time, negatively affect our health. Jeff Jeffries[30].

Cell Phones

There is strong suspicion, based on the existing science, that cell phones can cause brain tumours, salivary gland tumours and eye cancer, as well as insomnia and fatigue. Many public health experts believe we will face an epidemic of cancers in the future resulting from the uncontrolled use of cell phones and the increased population exposure to Wi-Fi and other wireless devices. David Carpenter[31].

Most of the twentieth century diseases of civilization, including cancer, cardiovascular disease, malignant neoplasms, diabetes, and suicide, are not just caused by lifestyle alone, these disease are now increasing in direct proportion to our increasing exposures to high technology electrical devices. Samuel Milham[32].

Electromagnetic pollution may be the most significant form of pollution human activity has produced in this century, all the more dangerous because it is invisible and insensible. Andrew Weil[33].

Microwave ovens

Microwaves break chemical and molecular bonds, and can literally rip atoms apart, disrupting the basic biochemical structures of life. It's no wonder foods cooked in such a way may become harmful to consume. Government and industry studies suggest they pose no threat, but a growing body of knowledge now contradicts those claims.

The Swiss scientist Hans Hertel[34], was the first to study microwave dangers, specifically how cooking degrades and depletes food of nutrients – an effect that shows up in study participants' blood samples. In the late 1980s, Hertel and seven fellow vegetarians locked themselves into a hotel room, where they performed a two-month "experiment" that consisted of eating foods prepared in the microwave and by other means. After two months of togetherness, Hertel emerged with a terrifying pronouncement: he had found changes that what "appear to indicate the initial stage of a pathological process such as occurs at the start of a cancerous condition" in the blood of the men who had eaten microwaved milk and vegetables.

When the microwave radiation destroys and deforms food molecules, new harmful compounds form (radio lytic compounds), which harm the body in many ways. The handful of studies that have been done generally agree, that microwaving food damages its nutritional value. (See Dangers of Microwave Ovens[35]).

Another study of microwave problems reported in the Medical journal, The Lancet[36], showed that when infant formula was microwaved for ten minutes, it altered the structure of its component amino acids, possibly resulting in functional, structural and immunological abnormalities.

(See How to minimise EMF Radiation in Part 7).

David Carpenter[37] is clear that it is time for fully independent studies, funded by those governmental agencies, whose charter is to protect its citizens, be undertaken, so that the truth about the very damaging health hazards of microwave and other sources of damaging radiation becomes clear and well known. This is all well supported by the work of Lloyd Morgan[38].

We are it seems now in an age of degenerative and man-made diseases. We may well be killing ourselves.

It's time to change the world and it begins now.

If we could give every individual the right amount of nourishment and exercise, not too little and not too much, we would have found the safest way to health.

Hippocrates

"Everyone has a doctor in him or her; we just have to help it in its work. The natural healing force within each one of us is the greatest force in getting well. Our food should be our medicine. Our medicine should be our food. But to eat when you are sick, is to feed your sickness."
– Hippocrates

Part 3: Food

To include a Part in this book, on the subject of food, will I am sure, invite controversy. There are so many other books written about one or more types of diet on what we should or should not eat, with the media coming out with the latest 'discovery', only to reverse their opinion at some later stage, and creating confusion and uncertainty. Notwithstanding, I have sought to bring together those aspects, which in my mind, are important to seriously consider.

Hippocrates knew a thing or two in healing the body, advocating that good health can be achieved through nutrition and a satisfactory way of life which includes a correct supply of air, food and drink. We can shorten or lengthen our existence, depending on the intake of these three components.

The advantage of being healthy is that it results in the generation of energy stored in our organs. Our body is innately intelligent and will always seek to find ways to heal and balance any harm from the bombardment of toxins that are invading our system. The harmful factors are not only pollutants and an unbalanced and nutritionally depleted food intake, but also the mismanagement of our emotions. It is quite possible to live until you are 125 and be in perfect health. (see 'The Blue Zones' – areas of the world where people live the longest[39]).

The Hunza tribe and inhabitants of the equatorial Andes, have a huge proportion of one hundred year olds, who maintain their enjoyment of life and their vitality. The secret of their extraordinary long lives and amazing good health, both physical and mental, is likely to be the result of their way of living; respectful of nature, have a frugal, yet nutritionally balanced diet and stress free lives. (The Hunza Tribes[40]).

When a few decades ago the first western doctors discovered this amazing longevity, they were equally amazed at the almost total absence of disease. Their resistance to infection and disease was proverbial as they were not apparently affected by cancer, diabetes or heart attacks. They also seemed not to decline with age, become weak, lose their teeth, their sight, or hearing. This is seen to be as a consequence of a simple physically hardworking way of life and an ability, when food is short, to fast for several weeks, before the harvest of fruit and vegetables arrives. They mainly restrict their calorie intake to 2,000 per day with excellent quality in terms of nutrition. The next factor for a long life is physical activity allowing toxins to be eliminated in sweat, and an increase in oxygen intake by breathing in clean unpolluted air. Dr Jean-Pierre Willem[41].

Natural biological life is seen by scientists to be at 120 years. This really begs the question as to why this is not happening in our western world.

Let us now consider some possible food related factors that are seen to be the cause of our health problems.

Fast Foods

There has been a vast rise in fast food shops and takeaways. These foods are very tempting because they save cooking and the food presented is very tasty.

One likely reason for the enjoyable taste is the addition of monosodium glutamate (MSG) a food additive, used specifically as a flavour enhancer. MSG is the sodium salt of the common amino acid glutamic acid. Glutamic acid is naturally present in our bodies and also occurs naturally in many foods, such as tomatoes and cheeses. WDDTY 19 Nov 2012[42]. It is also a food additive and used as a flavour enhancer. It is generally associated as being present in Chinese food. However it is also added to thousands of the foods we regularly eat, especially if the majority of your food is processed or you eat in restaurants that add this. Most commercially packaged food products like chips contain MSG.

Ingredients like hydrolysed protein, autolyzed yeast, and sodium caseinate are all pseudonyms for MSG. Some people find that consuming MSG, especially in large quantities, can trigger various side effects and symptoms, including – but not limited to – headaches, nausea, dizziness, rapid or irregular heartbeat, flushing and excessive sweating, skin rash, numbness, intense thirst, lethargy or sleepiness, ringing ears or tingling in the mouth. Danilo Alfaro[43].

Is MSG Safe? Although many people report the above allergic symptoms to MSG, scientists say it is safe to eat. As MSG greatly enhances the taste of savoury foods, this accounts for its heavy use. MSG is also a popular ingredient in Asian recipes and can be found in the spice aisle of most grocery stores. Peggy Trowbridge Filippone[44].

The vitamin and nutritional quality of many convenient and processed foods, is typically far below and differs substantially, from that of the nutritional density of fresh organic whole foods. Organically grown grains, harvested from land unadulterated by the use of pesticides, and animals raised on 100 percent organic grass from fertile ground, will then supply us with nutritionally high produce in the form of grains, meat, milk and eggs. Organic foods are significantly higher in vitamin C, vitamin E, polyphenols and total antioxidants, especially in regenerative organic systems. Poor nutrition and lack of vitamins go hand in hand with disease.

As a rough guide, in order to maintain her weight a woman needs to eat about 2000 calories per day and a man 2500, depending of course, on physical activity. School-age children need about 1,600 to 2,500 calories per day. Children between the ages of 5 and 6 need 41 calories per pound of body weight, and those between 7 and 11 should have 32 calories per pound.

However with the increasing uptake of meals from fast food shops with high amounts of trans fats, refined carbs and calorie content, is it any wonder that the nation and our children are overweight? As a consequence because of its widespread prevalence, obesity is now looked upon as a disease.

The state of obesity occurs when there is an excess intake of calories compared to requirements, often associated with the consumption of sugar and toxic foods. This automatically sets in motion a series of events by the immune system, as it attempts to manage the toxins and bring the body back into homeostasis (balance & wellbeing). This process leads in turn to the release of various hormones, which if persistent over time, can result in heart disease, liver and kidney failure, learning and behavioural disorders, cancers, food allergies, asthma. In fact a whole host of chronic diseases.

Other toxic substances being taken into our bodies and subsequently leading to disease, include pesticide residues, antibiotics, hormone-disruptors, salmonella, campylobacter, listeria, e-coli, slaughterhouse waste and a growing list of other horrors in our food, food packaging and drinking water.

Trans Fats

Artificial Trans fats are created through the process of hydrogenation of plant-based oils and animal fats, when these liquid fats are turned into soft solids such as shortening or margarine.

While the dangers of trans fats (vegetable oils which have undergone a chemical process of hydrogenation which alters their chemical structure), are now becoming widely recognized, the recommended replacement with vegetable oils – may actually be even more harmful, because when heated, vegetable oils can degrade into extremely toxic oxidation products, including cyclic aldehydes, which causes severe inflammation and may also damage your gastrointestinal tract. Trans fats can increase LDL ("bad") cholesterol, says James Marin[45], R.D., a dietitian based in Orange County, California and it also lowers the HDL ("good") cholesterol, whose function is to mop up excess fat lingering in the blood.

Removing trans fats from your diet can promote heart health. Concomitant with low-fat diets becoming the cultural norm, heart disease rates have soared, clearly demonstrating saturated fat is not a contributing factor. Studies have confirmed that higher HDL cholesterol levels are associated with better health and longer life. Saturated fat and cholesterol have been wrongfully vilified as the culprits of heart disease for more than six decades. Meanwhile, research has repeatedly identified refined carbs, sugar and trans fats found in processed foods as the real enemy. The first scientific evidence linking trans fats to heart disease while exonerating saturated fats was published in 1957 by the late Fred Kummerow[46].

Unfortunately, Kummerow's science was overshadowed by Ancel Keys in *A Multivariate Analysis of Death and Coronary Heart Disease*[47], which linked saturated fat intake with heart disease. The rest, as they say, is history. Later reanalysis revealed that cherry-picked data was responsible for creating Keys' link, but by then the saturated fat myth was already firmly entrenched.

Keys' biased research launched the low-fat myth and reshaped the food industry for decades to come. As saturated fat and cholesterol were shunned, the food industry switched to using trans fats (found in margarine, vegetable shortening and partially hydrogenated vegetable oils) and sugar instead.

The conclusion is that refined carbs, sugar and trans fats found in processed foods are the primary dietary culprits causing heart disease, not saturated fat or cholesterol. Nina Teicholz[48].

High blood levels of homocysteine[49], rather than cholesterol, is a preferred indicator for heart disease.

Saturated Fats

Saturated fat plays a key role in sustaining cardiovascular health. It is required for calcium to be effectively incorporated into bone and to protect the liver from alcohol and medications. Your brain is mainly made of fat and cholesterol. Certain saturated fats, particularly those found in butter, lard, coconut oil and palm oil, function directly as messengers that influence metabolism, including such critical jobs as the appropriate release of insulin. Other saturated fats found in butter and coconut oil play key roles in immune health. It is the preferred fuel for your heart, and used as a source of fuel during energy expenditure. It is an antiviral, antiplaque and an antifungal agent, and is an addition to good health. Dr Mercola[49].

Soy Milk

Soy milk or soymilk is a plant-based drink produced by soaking and grinding soybeans, boiling the mixture, and filtering out remaining particulates. It is a stable emulsion of oil, water, and protein. It is a good source of protein, vitamin A, B12, vitamin D, and potassium... Soy milk contains almost as much protein as cow's milk, yet is lower in calories than whole milk and comparable to skim milk. It contains no cholesterol, which is seen by the medical profession, important for those with heart conditions.

However there are some side effects that need to be considered, affecting; fertility in women — causing heavy periods; endocrine disruption — causing loss of libido; high risk of bladder cancer; harmful for pancreas; obstructs absorption of various minerals — increasing chances of blood clotting; leads to hypothyroidism; causes gastrointestinal discomfort; endometrial cancer and asthma. (See — Soy Side Effects[50]).

Using soy protein in moderate amounts benefits your health, while excessive intake could leave you with mild or aggressive side effects. As always seek advice from an authority before using this product on a regular basis.

Sweeteners

Aspartame hides behind brand names such as NutraSweet, Equal, Spoonful, and Equal-Measure. Our bodies have evolved to efficiently use the energy sources available in nature. Aspartame[51] is not a natural compound; it is a synthetic chemical, composed of the amino acids phenylalanine and aspartic acid, with a methyl ester. When consumed, the methyl ester breaks down into methanol, which may be converted into formaldehyde. This can have a negative effect on your nervous system so much so that Aspartame is categorized as a neurotoxin (brain poison). It causes a reduction in serotonin and dopamine — chemicals which are very critical in operating a healthy brain. Our modern food intake is bombarded by chemicals that our bodies have never seen before and decades of science points to serious health consequences.

Another sweetener is Splenda, but it is anything but splendid. It is a chemical containing sucralose, a chemical which alters the amount and quality of those beneficial microbes that hang out in your belly (the same ones found in yogurt) by 50% or more. "Alteration in bacterial counts is associated with weight gain and obesity" says Dr Susan Shiffman[52].

Many people bake with Splenda to reduce the calories in a recipe, but the sucralose it contains, decomposes during baking, and releases potentially toxic compounds called chloropropanols – a class of chemical compounds which can affect your body's responses. Sucralose can also alter insulin responses and blood sugar levels which has been associated with inflammatory bowel disease, and may even alter genes, the researchers note. Other research cited in *Journal of Toxicology and Environmental Issues*[52], found that sugar substitutes containing sucralose are linked to type 2 diabetes, heart disease, metabolic syndrome, and obesity. So if you want something sweet, your best option is regular sugar in moderation (not sucralose) – no more than 100 calories, or 6 added teaspoons a day, as per the American Heart Association's recommendations[53].

Fruit Drinks.

Fruit juice is often perceived as healthy. That is understandable, given that it is natural and has the word "fruit" in it. However what many people fail to realize is that fruit juice is also loaded with sugar which adds to their calorie intake and where labelled 'diet' they contain aspartame or similar sweeteners. A study published in the Journal of Respirology Feb 2013[54] reveals that soft drink consumption is also associated with lung and breathing disorders including asthma and chronic obstructive pulmonary disease (COPD).

Energy and sport drinks also contain caffeine which acts as a central nervous system stimulant. When it reaches your brain, the most noticeable effect is alertness, however caffeine can cause, nervousness and restlessness, insomnia, stomach irritation, nausea and vomiting, increased heart rate and respiration, and other side effects.

People who consume soft drinks such as Coke experience a 48%

increase risk of heart attack and stroke, compared to people who do not either drink the sodas at all, or do not drink them every day. The pleasurable 'high' from the caffeine can also lead to addiction.

Caffeine in Coke and similarly in coffee, can reduce calcium in bones, resulting in osteoporosis, leading to possible fractures at some stage. It is also very acidic, being only one point higher on the pH scale than battery acid. Consequently, it can clean surfaces and many now find it is often better than many toxic household cleaners, such as a toilet cleaner, being as effective as bleach. It can also be used to clean oil stains from a garage floor and is undeniably a very useful product. The key is to use it for purposes that do not include drinking! See all References[55].

Conclusion

Avoid food that has been chemically added or sprayed and if this is not possible, at least wash them. The best thing is to buy organic – vegetables, meat & fruit. (See Organic Food – in Part 5).

Avoid food that has been processed or prepared in a fast food outlet with their high calories, trans fats and chemically laden preparations.

Cook meals in the home where you know how it is being prepared.

We need meat for our health but where possible avoid animal meat that has been subjected to hormone injections and fish which have been farm raised, as they are fed a diet of antibiotics and pesticides.

Healthy eating can be simplified into four words: 'Just Eat Real Food'. But this is easier said than done when we are surrounded by slippery marketing claims about "all natural" health foods, which actually have chemicals added.

The sun, rain and soil create everything we enjoy. Respect the beauty of nature as it lies at the heart of everything we do.

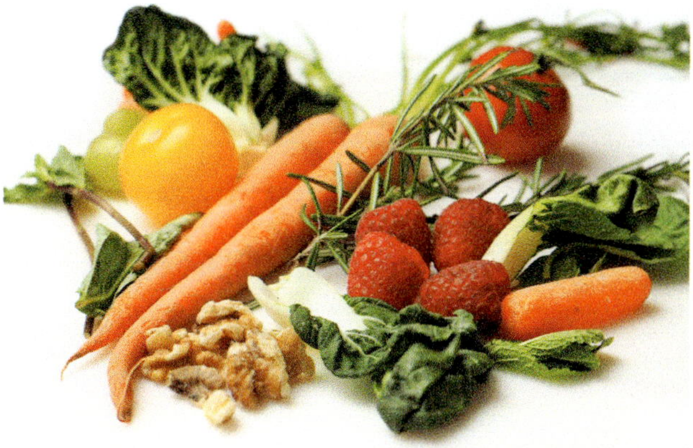

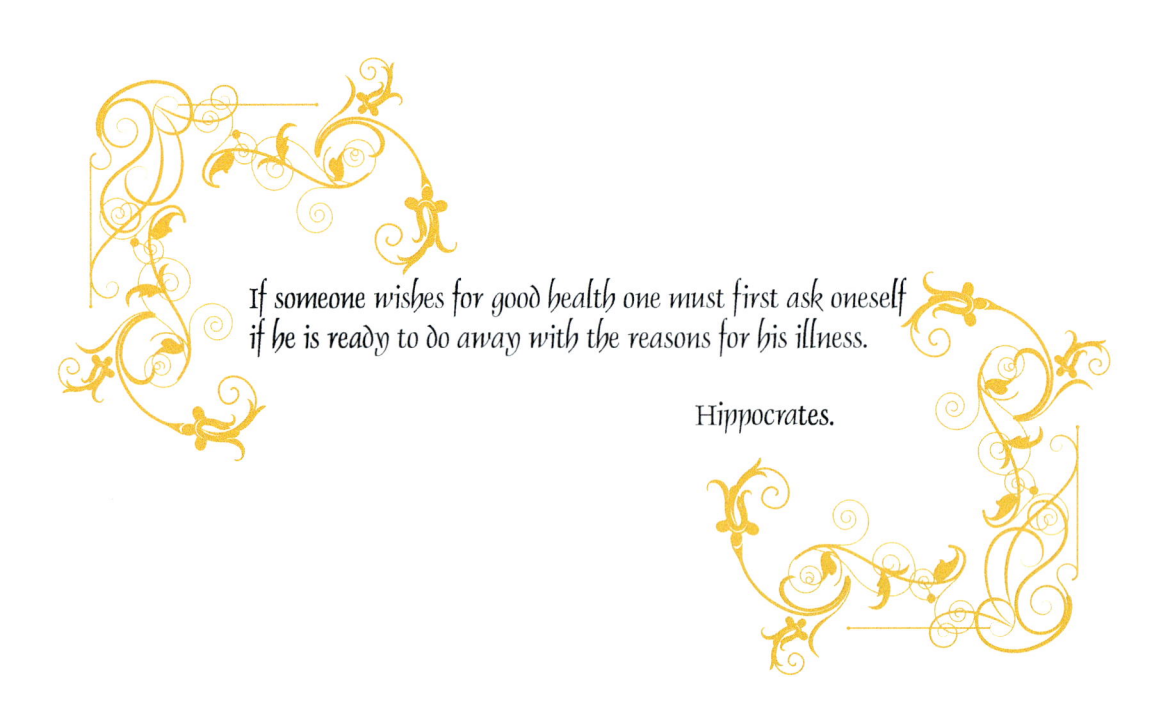

If someone wishes for good health one must first ask oneself
if he is ready to do away with the reasons for his illness.

Hippocrates.

Part 4: Addictions

Below I have identified practices that have real adverse health effect on our lives. As these may still not be fully appreciated, I have gathered as much information as possible to show how they can affect our health.

Smoking

In the short-term smoking is enjoyable for those who indulge, as it stimulates the pleasure part of our brain that lets us know when something is enjoyable, this then reinforces the desire for us to perform the same pleasurable action again and again. People become addicted to the drug nicotine contained in the tobacco. As with all addictions, this creates a compulsive need to satisfy their cravings with regular doses. (Lung Association Newfoundland & Labrador[56]).

Nicotine is powerful stuff. It crosses the blood-brain barrier and messes with our dopamine pathways, which have an effect on the brain. After years of smoking, those pathways get altered. In other words, smoking can lead to physical changes in our brain.

As well as nicotine, there are more than 4,000 chemicals in tobacco smoke. On inhalation, these cancer-causing chemicals travel throughout a smoker's bloodstream reaching many different organs of the body and encouraging the development of cancer cells in the body. With this suppression of the immune system there is consequently a reduction in its ability to get rid of these chemicals, which therefore remain within the body increasing with each cigarette.

The degree, to which people see the cumulative risk, raises important questions. It is widely held that cigarette smoking reflects a rational choice and that people are well informed about the risks. However, Krosnick[57] and colleagues rebut the tobacco companies' claim that beginner smokers understand the risks. When undertaking their research and exploring the risks smokers face in his study, they looked at: their regret at taking up the habit, the nature of their addiction, the effects of advertising, and believe it or not, some smokers' held the belief that they were immune to any dangers from smoking. The risks of smoking accumulate one cigarette at a time and the above study worryingly suggests that a higher percentage of adolescent smokers see no health risk from smoking the next cigarette, or even from smoking regularly for the first few years.

With the intake of tobacco smoke for each cigarette, some tar is deposited in the lungs. Our lungs are lined with tiny hairs (cilia) that help 'sweep' germs, dust and other air pollutants out. It is harder for these hairs to move if the lungs are coated with tar and so their capacity is reduced. In time this accumulation can lead to Chronic Obstructive Pulmonary Disease (COPD), with life changing breathing difficulties.

The main factor is the presence of carbon monoxide which then binds itself to haemoglobin in the bloodstream and reduces the oxygen being carried around the body. This is why pregnant mothers are urged to completely give up smoking, as this lack of oxygen not only distresses the baby even at the first intake but also has an impact on its growth. Mothers who smoke during pregnancy give birth to smaller babies because their development is curtailed or restricted. They have a disadvantaged start in life, not just because they are smaller than they should be but also because after birth, they will crave the nicotine they have been getting through the mother's blood stream during their development. The placental barrier has no means to prevent this. Consequently they will present as a very distressed baby.

The chances of developing lung cancer are also affected by how much an individual smokes and for how long. However, many smokers will state that they know of an elderly relative who smoked all their life and still lived to a ripe old age. They are, as a consequence, reluctant to take any notice of the doom and gloom they hear regarding the dangers of cigarette smoking especially as they find the habit enjoyable. It soon becomes a crutch to be used at every available stress situation. But it's a complete myth that smoking helps you to relax. The reality is that smoking actually increases anxiety and tension. Smokers are more likely to develop depression or anxiety disorder over time than non-smokers and cutting out cigarettes triggers a big improvement in mood, as those who have broken the habit, have found.

Everyone has a choice in what they do with their body, to care or not to care. Patients who go to the Doctors surgery for cigarette smoking related problems, will have, either not fully appreciated the damage they were causing, or chose to put that information aside, thinking "it won't happen to me". Accepting and acknowledging that they are to blame is essential.

Vaping

Vaping is controversial. Research results demonstrated that vaping had led to no change in heart function at all and that e-liquid is far less toxic than tobacco smoke, with no evidence of nitrosamines (a cancer causing substance found in tobacco) in e-cigarettes. (See Vaping 1[58]) However there is strong evidence to suggest that these devices may actually expose users to toxic chemicals of lead, chromium and even arsenic and in particular substances, with known carcinogenic properties. (See Vaping 2[59]).

Alcohol

There are so many views on this subject. Moderate alcohol use has possible health benefits, but it's not risk-free. It sounds like a mixed message, as drinking alcohol may offer some health benefits, especially for your heart. It is really possible to enjoy alcohol by keeping it at a moderate level. This means that for healthy adults up to one drink a day for women of all ages and men older than age 65, and up to two drinks a day for men age 65 and younger. On the other hand, too much alcohol may increase your risk of health problems and damage your heart.

We need to help our immune system and prevent avoidable problems such as a risk of liver disease, heart disease, sleep disorders, depression, stroke, bleeding from the stomach, several types of cancer, problems managing diabetes, high blood pressure, and other conditions. Heavy drinkers have a greater risk of liver disease, including cirrhosis, hepatitis, heart disease, kidney damage, sleep disorders, nutritional deficiency, depression, stroke, bleeding from the stomach, sexually transmitted infections from unsafe sex, and several types of cancer including breast cancer. They may also have problems managing diabetes, high blood pressure, and other conditions. Women who drink during pregnancy also run the risk of damage to their child by curtailing the development to various organs especially in the first three months of pregnancy, as this is the vital time of formation.

Hospital visits for alcohol poisoning doubled in six years, with the highest rate among females aged 15 to 19, in a detailed report as far back as Dec 2015, by the BBC[60]. They cause an inordinate amount of disruption in A&E departments with verbal abuse and actual physical harm to staff and others waiting to be seen.

Alcohol is not imposed upon people so the decision on how much to consume is to do with the mental state of each person. Only that person, who may need help, can effect a change. Alcoholics Anonymous (AA) is a fellowship of men and women who share their experience, their strengths and hopes with each other, that they may solve their common problem and help others to recover from alcoholism. The only requirement for membership is a desire to stop drinking. There are no dues or fees for AA membership.

Illegal Drugs

All known illegal and addictive drugs act on the brain to produce their euphoric effects, creating a compelling need. Not only that, but they contain chemicals that tap into the communication system of the brain, interfering with the way neurons normally send, receive, and process information. These particular chemicals are also capable of real damage to the heart, and other important organs. This personal lifestyle choice, creates a great health burden on the individual and a cost to the Health and Social Services. In addition the immune system is compromised when it has to deal with the chemicals contained in the drugs. Although there's no universal definition for drug addiction, this condition is often defined by a compulsive need to seek and obtain the drug of choice over all other considerations. Addiction is also characterised by the dangers that it presents to the user, including the danger of physical illness, the threat of violence, exposure to crime, the destruction of personal relationships and the loss of personal integrity.

In addition, repeated drug use leads to changes in the function of multiple brain circuits that control the pleasures/reward part of the brain as well as, stress, decision-making, impulse control, learning and memory, and other functions. Some can cause more damage, leading to seizures, strokes, and by having a toxic effect on the cells of the brain, means that it will not function in a rational way. These changes make it harder for those with an addiction, to experience pleasure in response to natural rewards – such as food, sex, or positive social interactions – or to manage the stress in their lives, control their impulses and be able make the healthy choice to stop drug seeking. It becomes a habit that is hard to kick due to the immediate pleasure experienced. Stopping can cause intense withdrawal symptoms, such as exhaustion, anxiety and paranoia, and may require professional help.

If you need treatment for drug addiction, you're entitled to NHS care in the same way as anyone else that has a health problem. Contact your GP who can put you in touch with local centres. With the right help and support plus your own determination, it is possible for you to get drug free and stay that way. There is a 12 Step rehabilitation program available which essentially works by treating the mind and the spirit, bringing about a change in thinking and perception. Those who have undertaken this have found it a life changer. (See Natural ways to beat addictions[61]).

The big difficulty with family members and friends living with someone who is addicted, from whatever cause, is that they are also likely to be affected and will experience stress in emotional, financial and physical ways. Their lives will always be disrupted to some degree, thus creating stress and illness for them. They need help and support as well.

Compulsive Buying Disorder

We are constantly bombarded with online, print, and media ads, such as "Shop till you drop" that justify and add credibility to this behaviour and reinforce the shopping mentality. The reward, to boost self-esteem, is highly addictive but when the urge to shop becomes uncontrollable, constantly spending beyond one's means, on things that are not needed, this is now seen as damaging as gambling or alcoholism – leading inevitably to financial poverty and stress.

Mobile Phones

We now need to include a comparatively new addiction – the use of iPads and smartphones – causing a fair degree of disruption.

Mobile phones and smart phone usage can now be seen as a dependence syndrome, where people feel anxious when disconnected from them. Some users even exhibit problematic behaviours related to substance use disorders, such as preoccupation with mobile communication, excessive money or time spent on mobile phones, use of mobile phones in socially or physically inappropriate situations such as walking in busy streets, while in charge of children or driving an automobile. This increased mobile communication leads to adverse effects on relationships, and even anxiety if separated from their mobile phone, for whatever reason. (See Journal of Natural Science, Biology and Medicine[62]).

This compulsive and dependant habit, which has burgeoned in the last few years, is changing society's communication in an unprecedented way. It is also the route taken by paedophiles for their grooming of young people. With the freedom of indiscriminate communication it is also being used for bullying behaviour, the consequence of which is emotionally destructive for the receiver. Addiction to one's mobile phones – leading to comparison of others' activities, compulsively needing to keeping in touch with so called 'friends', being compelled to play online games – has now taken over from social lifestyle activities, which lack full and meaningful support from face to face contact with peers and even family. Life is increasingly being experienced through a false and virtual world. Stress can be the only outcome.

Gambling

Gambling is the wagering of money or something of value (referred to as "the stakes") on an event with an uncertain outcome, with the primary intent of winning money or material goods. Most people gamble at some point in their lives, but for some, gambling can become a serious addiction. For the vast majority of people, gambling entails putting a bet on a sports match now and again or entering the weekly lottery draw. However more than 2 million people in the UK are either problem gamblers or at risk of addiction. The Guardian August 2017[63].

Gambling is very addictive, the adrenaline rush associated with the possibility of pulling off a big win is often described by gamblers as an unbeatable feeling and it is easy to see how people get hooked on gambling, especially as they now have the means to access these gambling outlets 24 hours a day, via the internet.

In addition there are many offers of 'Get Rich Quick' schemes. Sharks prey on the vulnerable, in many and ingenious ways, luring them into parting with their money. The outcome of gambling is likely to result in stress and ill health, not just for the gambler but the immediate family.

In recent years, the number of people experiencing problems with gambling has increased, due to economic troubles associated with the global recession. It is estimated that around 450,000 people in the UK are suffering from a gambling addiction. Where this impinges on the family budget, it leads to financial hardship and consequently damaging effects on family, personal life or recreational pursuits. (See: Gambling Addiction and treatment)[64].

> *"There are two ways of meeting difficulties: you alter the difficulties, or you alter yourself to meet them".*
> —Phyllis Bottoms

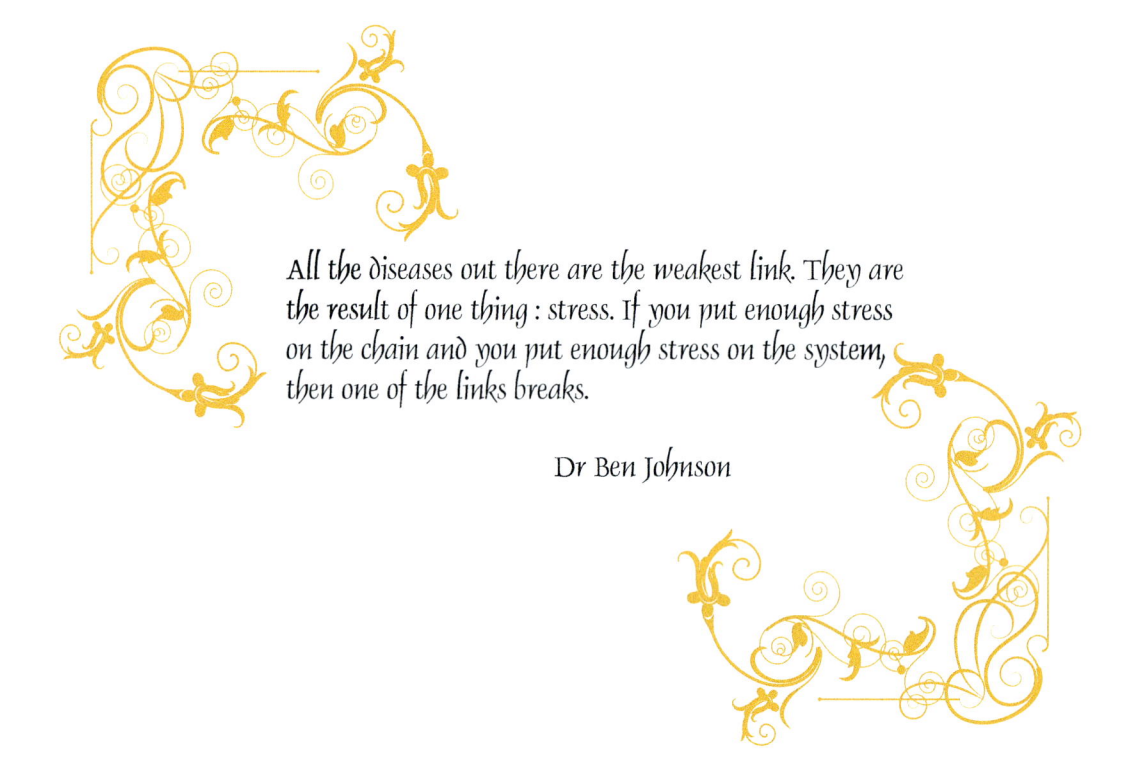

All the diseases out there are the weakest link. They are the result of one thing: stress. If you put enough stress on the chain and you put enough stress on the system, then one of the links breaks.

Dr Ben Johnson

Part 5: Active Ways to Maintain our health

From all of the above it would seem that we have moved into a manmade disease culture. What can we do about this?

Fortunately, Dr Bergman[65] discusses how 97% of diseases can be prevented and cured outside of the established medical allopathic model of healthcare – a system in which medical doctors and other healthcare professionals such as nurses, pharmacists and therapists, treat symptoms and diseases using drugs, radiation, or surgery.

There is a growing sense that the belief system of this medical allopathic model of healthcare is beginning to shift to a more comprehensive approach towards healing that supports the body's natural systems. This is long overdue.

We can now, with some relief, move into the many and varied ways which can help us to maintain our health and prevent disease in the first place. "Prevention is better than cure".

Water

At birth, water accounted for nearly 80 percent of your body weight and accounts for up to as much as 70 percent in an adult body. This has enormous consequences. Pure water holds much wisdom and when exposed to beautiful music and words depicting 'gratitude' it responds favourably, giving good energy. How is this so?

The author Masaru Emoto[66] has spent a great part of his life experimenting with what water can do for us. His Book "The Hidden Messages in Water" goes into great detail about this. He has demonstrated that when water is given positive love and gratitude then lovely crystals can form, showing that water responds to the thoughts and vibrations we give out. Classical music also has this effect.

In contrast when subjected to angry words such as 'stupid', beautiful crystals will not form, and become a mess of images. If we are surrounded by harsh words or disturbing sounds then it is reasonable to conclude that our body water will be affected and we will be experiencing some internal distress in response to the negative words or sounds around us.

Society deluges us all the time with negative images through television, movies magazines and newspapers and we don't realise it most of the time. It seems therefore we are affected twofold; emotionally with stress from the hormones which get released in stressful situations and from our own body water.

If we can, as much as is possible, avoid being around harsh words or any negative experiences, then we are walking the path of greater inner happiness and peace. Happiness has its own rewards, as this prompts the release of the hormone serotonin, beneficial to feeling happy and content.

So an important aspect of this is "are you happy"? Do you have a sense of peace in your heart and a feeling of security in your life.

Let us now examine our water more closely:

Dr. Allen E Banik[67] explains how water functions in the body, what the effects of myriad pollutants in drinking water are and their contribution to disease and he shows the benefit of drinking the purest of waters.

We are consuming approximately 450 pounds of inorganic minerals from tap water in our lifetime. The pollutants, in much of our water, include chemicals from industry plus commercial chemical fertilisers, weed killers and pesticides, all washed into streams by run off. Any water that has come from rivers and over the earth has also collected these inorganic minerals.

Previous work largely focused on plastic pollution in the oceans, suggesting people are also eating micro plastics via contaminated seafood. Now tests show that billions of people globally are drinking water contaminated by plastic particles, with 83% of samples found to be polluted as current standard water treatment systems do not filter out all the micro plastics and humans are at risk of drinking micro plastics in their drinking water. Dr Anne Marie Mahon[68]. The main sources include; the plastics manufacturing and recycling industries, landfills, septic tanks, urban wastewater treatment plants, and the sewage sludge/bio solids derived from such plants.

> *"Urban wastewater treatment plants were identified as one of the largest point sources of micro plastics, in the current study and were found to be receiving micro plastics from a number of different sources."*
>
> —Paul Melia[69]

Bottled water may not provide a micro plastic-free alternative to tap water, as particles were also found in a few samples of commercial bottled water tested in the US.

There are some who might still have the false impression that their tap water, including water produced by home filtration systems as well as bottled water is "pure", but it isn't. Tap water is loaded with many types of suspended pollutants, chemicals, toxins plastics and other contaminants. Bottled water is usually just plain tap water that has been minimally filtered to get rid of the bad odour and taste. Even water produced by reverse osmosis is not pure either.

Boiling water is very often advised if there is a problem with our water supply but boiling does not remove any of these inorganic particles. We are obtaining our essential minerals from our drinking water, but at the cost of absorbing all the other inorganic material. This is a very important point. Plants actually feed off and need inorganic minerals and then they convert them into organic minerals. These essential minerals are obtainable from plants and foods such as, fruits, nuts, grains, vegetables and meats and particularly sea and rock salts and these are necessary for us.

So what effect does the build-up of these inorganic minerals have on our bodies and subsequently our health? To put it simply, they clog up different parts of the body depending on the individual. This inevitably leads to illness requiring medical intervention. One way, Dr Banik[70] asks us to consider, in order to prevent this build up, is by drinking distilled water. This is pure water, containing no deposits of any kind. It will begin to flush out the build-up of these inorganic particles and chemicals in our bodies, thus freeing us of possible health problems as we get older. We can distil our own water at home. Dr. Banik goes on to say: "Imagine one possible common cause for nearly all diseases? Can it be that arthritis, enlarged hearts, kidney stones, gall stones, arteriosclerosis, glaucoma, diabetes etc. all stem from this one common cause – our water?"

A further important point to note is that our drinking water, in addition to the chemicals and pollution from the pesticides sprayed on the land for the crops, also contains the drugs that are expelled by our urine. Not all of these are cleared by our sewerage system and so they are recycled and returned to our bodies via our tap water.

It is also known that a possible cause of premature aging is due to an over acid and dehydrated body. A theory held by Dr Zach Bush[71] is that a large percent of us are running around really profoundly dehydrated and over time this can result in inflammatory and autoimmune conditions. Intracellular hydration is key for the prevention of such diseases. However drinking lots of water is not the total picture. When we talk about hydration, it is not about putting more water in our body, but actually getting the water inside the cells of our body, which is where the effective process of toxic elimination takes place.

So how do we move water from our intestinal lining actually into our cells? This is achieved only through the restoration of our gut membrane by improving the electrical charge within our cells. Dr Zach Bush advocates using a mineral supplement that creates a firewall against toxins entering the gut wall, helping create a biological environment for "good" gut bacteria to grow and flourish in order to support improvement of overall health.

Himalayan Rock Salt

Himalayan rock salt is also known as pink rock salt because of its distinctive pale pink colour. Mined in Pakistan, Himalayan rock salt is a naturally occurring salt, rich in a number of minerals. Himalayan rock salt can be harvested as large blocks, such as for cooking slabs or making rock salt lamps, or it can be crushed into medium and small pieces. It can also be ground up at home in a salt grinder to use in cooking, much like regular sea salt. It is organic compliant and can be used in organic products.

According to Dr Helen Smith[72] of the Auckland Holistic Centre, the high mineral content of Himalayan salt has numerous health benefits. In addition, Dr Smith states that a natural salt such as Himalayan is better than table salt, which is treated with chemicals and anti-caking agents. Along with sodium, Himalayan salt has high quantities of organic phosphorous, calcium, potassium, iron, magnesium, zinc, selenium, copper, bromine, zirconium and iodine. All of these occur naturally, so the mineral content available in rock salt is readily absorbed and healthful.

Organic Food

Essential vitamins and minerals are higher in many organic foods. On average, organic food contains increased levels of many key nutrients which are essential for human health, although the levels are dropping.

Organic food doesn't contain food additives which have been linked to health problems such as heart disease, asthma, osteoporosis, migraines, food allergies and hyperactivity.

Pesticides are routinely used in conventional farming. Residues of these pesticides are regularly found in a high percentage of fruit and vegetables, and in 2004 the European Commission stated that a risk to human health cannot be ruled out anymore.

There is growing concern about the high use of antibiotics on farm animals and the possible risk to health being passed on by the consumption of these by humans. Antibiotic use in farm animals is seen now to threaten human health.

Those of you who are interested and searching for ways to boost your immune system with foods, I have included a few of the many books on this. (see Further Reading).

Food Supplements

It is now a well-known fact that our soil has less of the vital minerals than hitherto. However it is advisable to seek the advice from a professional and trained nutritionist prior to any self-administration with any conditions we may be concerned about.

Two natural and essential supplements I shall mention here are: natural plant based real Vitamin C found in fruits and vegetables. Please note that the Vitamin C supplement, commonly known as ascorbic acid is a chemical and depletes true Vitamin C. Robert Thompson[73].

The other important supplement is Vitamin D which is essential for bone health, for the absorption of calcium and the prevention of rickets in children and osteomalacia in adults. They include calciferol (vitamin D2) and cholecalciferol (vitamin D3). Vitamin D3 is mainly obtained from the sun when our bare skin is exposed to sunlight and is essential in supporting our immune system for many conditions.

In the midst of summer, there's plenty of daily sunlight to boost vitamin D levels in your body. The challenge lies in balancing skin protection from sun overexposure, while reaping vitamin D's health benefits. Concerned about skin cancer risks and sun-aging, many health authorities continue to warn against any outdoor sun unless you're wearing sunblock or sunscreen.

Ideally, people should get enough vitamin D from their food. However, that's difficult to do. Many folks don't get enough of the nutrient from dietary sources like fatty fish and fortified milk.

Vitamin D is a fat-soluble vitamin. Mother Nature paired foods rich in vitamin D with the healthy fats which are required for the absorption of this nutrient. For example, yolks from pasture-raised hens are a good source of fat-soluble vitamins A, D and K2. The beneficial saturated fats found in the egg yolks allow the body to absorb the fat-soluble vitamins. Vitamin D can also be obtained from the dairy produce of grass-fed cows and also cod liver oil.

Researchers now believe low vitamin D levels in winter leave you more susceptible to colds, flu and serious diseases such as osteoporosis, diabetes, and multiple sclerosis, as well as many forms of cancer and heart disease.

See a full explanation and the findings of an international research project called "D Action Project"[74] which is showing how essential it is, in supporting our immune system and how lack of vitamin D is responsible for a number of other health problems hitherto unknown. It is worth looking at, to fully understand the importance and the consequences to our health where there is a lack of vitamin D, especially for countries such as the UK which are in the northern hemisphere with insufficient sunshine. (See also: The British Association of Dermatologists[75]).

Your GP is able to test your level of vitamin D which needs to be at a level of 40 to 60 nanograms per millilitre. It is projected that the incidence of many diseases could be reduced by 20–50% or more, if the occurrence of vitamin D deficiency and insufficiency were eradicated by increasing vitamin D intakes through increased UVB exposure, fortified foods or supplements. It is also worth noting that vitamin K2 is necessary to help to move calcium into the proper areas in your body, keeping it in the bones and out of the arteries.

Exercise

We are all told that exercise is good, but why exactly?

Physical inactivity is a major risk factor for coronary heart disease. All regular physical activity can without question improve your muscle strength and boost your endurance. It will deliver oxygen and nutrients to your tissues and help your cardiovascular system work more efficiently. When your heart and lung health improve, you have more energy to tackle daily chores and create a sense of satisfaction. It also helps your bones maintain density and thus help prevent osteoporosis. (CMAJ. JAMC[76]).

Physical activity stimulates various brain chemicals – endorphins – that interact with the receptors in your brain and trigger a positive feeling in the body leaving you feeling happier and more relaxed. All exercise whatever type; helps prevent or manage a wide range of health problems and concerns, including stroke, heart disease, diabetes, depression, a number of types of cancer and arthritis. It also promotes better sleep, allowing you to be refreshed and enjoy the day.

Several biological mechanisms may be responsible for the reduction in the risk of chronic disease and premature death associated with undertaking regular physical activity. For instance, routine physical activity has been shown to improve body composition by reducing abdominal adiposity and improving weight control. It increase high-density lipoprotein HDL (good cholesterol) and decreases low-density lipoprotein LDL (bad cholesterol). It reduces blood pressure, reduces systemic inflammation through the reduction of C-reactive protein levels – the inflammatory cause of disease. It can also decrease blood coagulation, thereby improving coronary blood flow. Each of these factors may explain directly or indirectly the reduced incidence of chronic disease and premature death among people who engage in routine physical activity. Donna E. Shalala[77].

Here are a number of exercises to explore:

Cycling

Cycling can help to protect you from serious diseases such as stroke, heart attack, some cancers, depression, diabetes, obesity and arthritis.

Riding a bike is healthy, fun and a low-impact form of exercise for all ages and it is easy to fit into your daily routine by riding to the shops, park, school or work. Two to four hours a week will achieve a general health improvement.

Dancing

If you are able to take up dancing this is usually done with others. The social benefits of belonging to a group of like-minded people will be beneficial for one's mental health and wellbeing, as this has been shown to reduce depression, anxiety, and stress and to boost self-esteem, body image, with an overall sense of well-being. These benefits are seen to last over time.

There are lots of different places where you can enjoy dancing, for example, at dance schools, social venues, community halls and in your own home. Dancing has become such a popular way to be active and keep fit, that most fitness clubs now offer classes.

Swimming

Every type of exercise has its selling points and with swimming, the fact that you're submerged in water means your bones and muscles are somewhat unshackled from the constraints of gravity. Swimming decreases arterial stiffness, a risk factor for heart trouble. As a sport, swimming keeps your heart rate up and takes some of the impact stress off your body. It is great for building endurance, muscle strength and cardiovascular fitness and in addition it tones muscles and builds strength. It also helps maintain a healthy weight, healthy heart and lungs.

Team sports of any nature

One of the health benefits of playing sports in a team is that it is an emotional, mental and physical adventure. You have the opportunity to learn what you're made of and to determine if you're a team player or a maverick. Through the participation in sports, friendships can develop with other team members – if you play safely and smartly. This can give you 'the feel good' factor from the support of your team. Such activity develops a great camaraderie with other members and by feeling accepted by them and belonging to a group, this can boost ones self-image, happiness, mental wellbeing and hence lead to overall health.

Walking/Gym

Taking a regular 30 minutes of brisk walking has been found to trigger the anti-aging process, while heading to the gym for a quick workout is one of the most common ways to aid mental and physical health as well as reducing stress and obesity. It has been found to trigger an anti-aging process that could add an additional three to seven years to your life and reduce the risk of heart disease and stroke by up to 27%, control high blood pressure, improve circulation, reduce bad cholesterol (LDL), and help increase good cholesterol (HDL).

Exercise also increases concentrations of norepinephrine, a chemical that can moderate the brain's response to stress. It is clear that exercise has many benefits from creating a general feeling of wellbeing to the prevention of a great many diseases.

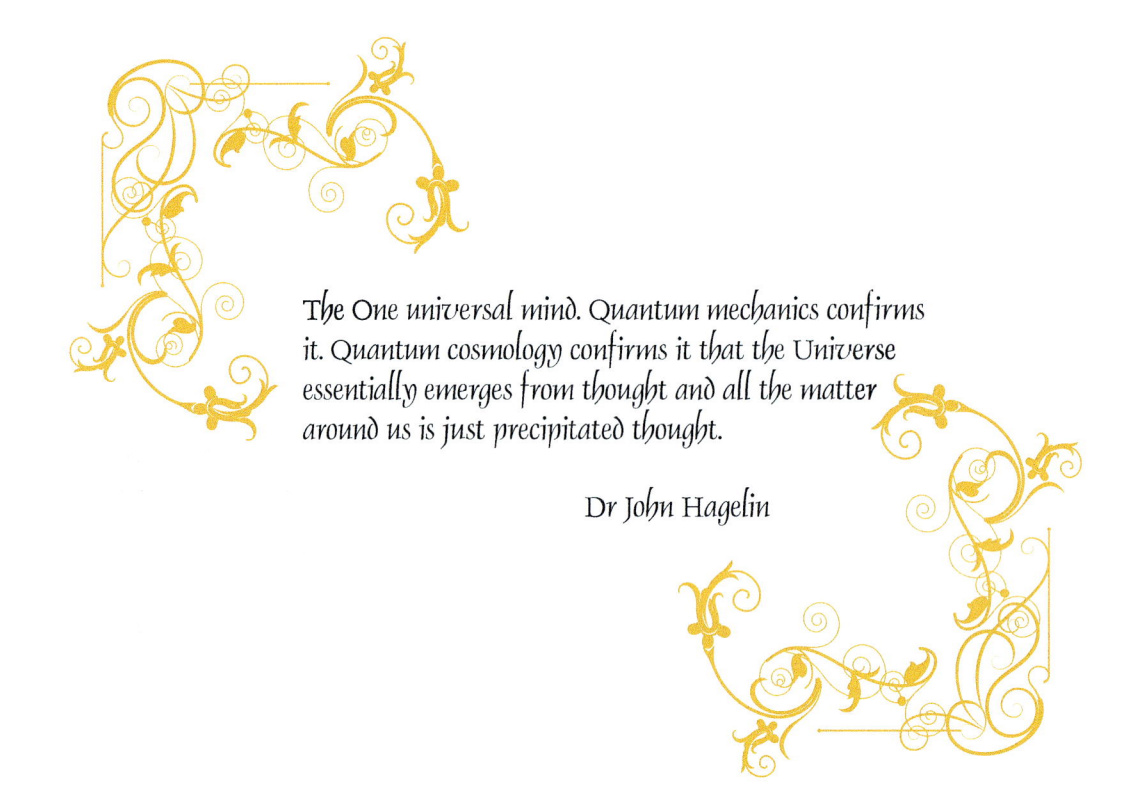

The One universal mind. Quantum mechanics confirms it. Quantum cosmology confirms it that the Universe essentially emerges from thought and all the matter around us is just precipitated thought.

Dr John Hagelin

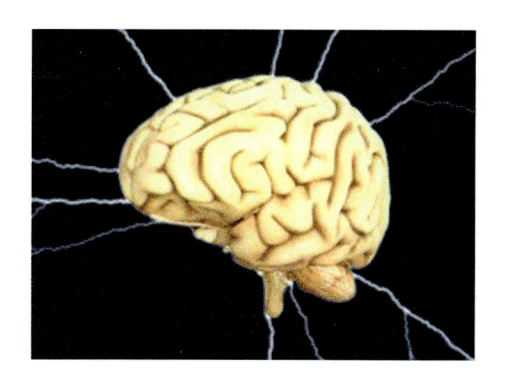

Part 6: Our Mind can Heal us

Much research has revealed the power of our subconscious minds. It is like a human computer, recording everything that has happened in our lives. The subconscious mind knows exactly what is going on with us, and how we can heal.

It is appropriate here to ask here, "what does it take to make a decision?" Three factors are needed: the ability to see a problem; the energy to focus on making a change; and the intention to choose how this can be carried out. These are sufficient to cause any individual or system to change, and to use that change to go in a particular direction. If any of these factors are missing, change is no longer possible, as the mind is not focussed on any determined path, a prerequisite of achievement.

In 1970, the late German physicist Fritz-Albert Popp[78] found that humans emit a tiny amount of photons, or light, from the DNA of every cell and that when medicine was applied to one part of the body, a great change in the amount of light was triggered in other more distant parts of the body. Popp came to realise that this light was a real communication channel within a living organism – a means of instantaneous signalling. His work affords us a real understanding that the body works as an exquisitely interconnected whole, what affects one part affects every other part simultaneously. To treat only one part as separate from all others is to invite calamity. (WDDTY Sept 2015[79]).

Energy medicine is becoming part of an expanding field of healing that does not involve the use of pharmaceutical drugs, conventional medical treatment, or even complimentary supplements. It is more powerful than anything ever discovered both by traditional and alternative medicine. For the first time, both traditional and alternative doctors agree that energy medicine is the most powerful, legitimate healing source ever found. Its use will also prevent the development of any further problems. Dr Alex Loyd[80].

Healing on an emotional level has knock-on effects on all other levels: a healthy emotional life and a balanced personality will allow your body to find its own natural state of health. Positive emotions create harmony in our heart rhythms, boosting the entire nervous system and positively affecting health at the physical and emotional level. WDDTY 2017[81].

Debbie Shapiro[82] has written a very good book "Your Body Speaks Your Mind" telling us how we can determine what our bodies are saying to us.

The most powerful drug of all may be your thoughts. Dr Joe Dispenza[83] discovered that what we think and feel has a profound effect on either activating or silencing our genes and the healing molecules within our bodies.

I am now introducing you to a world of health, which is not damaging to our immune system, and which not only enhances our wellbeing, but aids in the prevention of illness and disease.

The Healing Code

According to Dr Alexander Loyd[84] there is a physical function built into the body that is capable of removing the source of 95% of all illness and disease. By activating this function the neuro-immune system can then heal whatever is wrong in the body. If the immune and healing systems of the body can heal any problems you have, then boosting our immune system will reduce illness and disease. These codes will put healing in your control by unlocking your own given health potential. Dr Bruce Lipton[85] – a renowned cell biologist – also supports the notion that at least 95 percent of illness and disease are caused by stress, with the remaining 5 percent being genetic.

It has to be said that stress and its affects are different from one person to another. The Healing Code can turn the immune system back on track whatever the causes. It is not necessary to understand any of those deep and hidden causes, or even know how the body works, for healing to take place. The Healing Code does not ever 'treat' any health issues. It only addresses the issues of the heart.

> *"Guard your heart above all else, for out of it are all the issues of life"*
> —Solomon. Proverbs 4:23

While working with the Healing Code, you will be working on the source of your health issues; the negative beliefs which are with you still, at a cellular level. Your body can then be healed and allow you to have the healthy life you want. The Healing Code is truly a very wonderful tool.

Be assured that the research carried out, also shows sound scientific evidence, that this method will enable your body to heal. The Heart Variable Rate (HRV)[86] is a recognised method to determine stress levels and is used in the research to evaluate the effectiveness of the Healing Code. It takes only a few minutes to learn this Healing Code, but the results will last a lifetime.

Meditation

Meditation[87] is a journey from external activity to inner silence. For most of your life, you may be busy doing things, but meditation will give you the opportunity to 'just be'. It is an opportunity to remember that in essence you are a human being rather than a human doing. Meditation guides you to quieter and quieter levels of the thinking process, until you slip beyond thought to discover the perfection that you are and have always been. This perfection has been hidden by layers of stress, fatigue, toxins, doubts, fears, and confusion. The mind is your consciousness – your thoughts, your feelings, your emotions, your personality, and your interpretation of reality. It is EVERYTHING that is aware and interactive with; it is the voice in your head.

Research has also shown that meditation works by stimulating the immune-system brain function regions[87]. As Dr Deepak Chopra[88] says, "Since your immune system responds to both negative and positive thoughts, meditation can create a positive mental environment for the immune system to flourish." He has combined the three pillars of the 5,000 year old timeless wisdoms of Meditation, Ayurveda, and Yoga at his centre.

Music

Because vibration is everything, our bodies are vibrating with energy and every vibration has its own frequency. We are all vibrating at different frequencies and therefore some frequencies may be right for others but not be the right ones for us. We need to find those that 'resonate' with us and make us feel good. Jonathan Goldman[89].

By exposing the mind and body to the various vibrational frequencies in music, you can easily achieve a greater sense of balance and deep healing. These frequencies align you with the rhythms and tones that form the basis of the universe which will facilitate the positive healing of broken DNA – a source of disease. Multiple other physical health benefits are achieved by listening to various frequencies.

At 528 hertz, the sound frequency of "love" has the most powerful healing frequency ever found! This frequency was used through the middle ages with miraculous effects, but somehow it was lost and then rediscovered by an Italian medical doctor in the 1960's. Dr Joseph Puleo[90]. Since then, it has been clinically tested and validated and attuned to different body organs including deep spiritual and emotional healing. A very pleasant and relaxing listening while at the same time supporting our natural health system and allowing healing to takes place.

Other Ancient Solfeggio Frequencies include:

396HZ For peace and wellbeing. Supports blood, liver, kidney function, bones and brain health.

417HZ Known to positively affect digestive and stomach issues, metabolism, prostate, gallbladder, headache and lower back problems.

444HZ Contains multiple benefits and is the master key that precipitates the other frequencies.

639HZ Positively affects the endocrine system especially the adrenal glands plus gallbladder issues.

741HZ Positively affects the immune system and cleanses viral, bacterial and fungal infections.

852HZ This is the spiritual frequency and connects us in worship. Michael S. Tyrell[91].

EFT

The Emotional Freedom Technique is a method of psychological acupressure which has a component that can optimise our emotional health. Emotional health is absolutely essential to our physical health – no matter how devoted to other sound lifestyle practices we are, such as diet and exercise.

It is based on the same energy meridians used in traditional acupuncture but without the needles. The technique involves tapping with the fingertips to create energy into specific meridians whilst at the same time voicing your desired state as a positive affirmation. It is thought to clear any emotional block in our body's bioenergetics system, by restoring a level of balance in our energy and in our mind. This optimises the magnetic energy force which normally flows unheeded through our bodies but which in times of stress, physical or mental, can become blocked. The outcome of any blocked energy means that some organs are 'starved' of this energy and will become dysfunctional over time. It is not necessary to 'believe' for this to work. It is a fact that when our meridians of energy flow well we are healthier, and the converse is also true.

Two basic methods are combined. The first is learning where and how to tap and the second is how to voice affirmative statements. These can be learnt quite easily to apply, when alone, privately, and generally it takes only a few minutes to learn.

If you are like many others, feeling trapped; caught in a cycle of emotional trauma; chronic physical pain; compulsions and addictions and want to change. Or perhaps you are just experiencing an empty feeling inside, and tired of feeling sad, depressed, anxious, discontented, and unwell. Or you are fed up with relinquishing the power over your health and happiness to others, and you would like to grow, flourish, and thrive, putting the past in the past – then EFT could be the path you could travel. This is seen to be the way in achieving the best in you, living a life that is filled with peacefulness, joy, fulfilment and health, from day to day and moment to moment. (See EFT Techniques)[92].

A critical truth to remember is that when doing this work, your persistent and consistent thoughts will eventually become your reality. Respect and love yourself for taking care of this our most precious gift – our Body, Mind and Spirit Energy.

Mind Management (The Chimp Paradox)

The Chimp Paradox book[93] outlines a mind management model that can help you become a happy, confident, healthier and more successful person.

Dr Steve Peters[94] explains the struggle that takes place within your mind and then shows how to apply this understanding to every area of your life, so you can: recognise how your mind is working, understand and manage your emotions and thoughts and become the person you would like to be.

The Chimp Mind Management Model is based on scientific facts and principles, which have been simplified into a workable model for easy use. It will help you to develop yourself and give you the skills, for example, to remove anxiety, have confidence and choose your emotions. The model will do this by giving you an understanding of the way in which your mind works and how you can manage it. It will help you to identify what is holding you back or preventing you from having a happier and more successful life.

Each chapter explains different aspects of how you function and highlights key facts for you to understand. There are also exercises for you to work with. By undertaking these exercises, you will see immediate improvements in your daily living and, over time, you will develop emotional skills and practical habits that will help you to become the person that you want to be, and live the life that you want to live. There are seven different areas to work on:

Your inner mind/Understanding and relating to others/Communication/The world in which you live/Your health/Your success/Your happiness.

Every form of healing has a place.

Dr John Demartini

Part 7: Home Supportive Equipment

I will now introduce you to some home treatment systems which help in enhancing your immune system. They need to be purchased but then they are available for your own use, as and when desired.

Air Ionisers

Places we find refreshing, such as mountains, waterfalls and seashores, have high concentrations of negative ions. It is no coincidence then, that this is where health resorts are traditionally situated.

When air is enriched with negative ions, the oxygen it contains is far more easily absorbed and used by our body – helping us feel refreshed and alert, and as our stress hormones are reduced, we sleep more soundly. It has been proven too, that negative ions help animals and plants grow strong and healthy.

Positive ions are usually carbon dioxide molecules and are understood to have a negative health effect on your body when you are exposed to them in excess and are believed to contribute to tiredness and a lack of energy, tension, anxiety and irritability.

Unfortunately, our modern-day homes and workplaces have also become chronic generators of potentially harmful positive ions. Positive ions in the air have even been investigated as a contributing factor for asthma and depression.

We now are able to install Air ionisers or Negative ion generators in our homes, clearing the positive ions in our rooms. They are cheap to run and can be left on safely for long periods when in residence. Many styles are available. The more powerful the ioniser, the more beneficial ions they can produce and the larger their range. Traffic pollutants can be reduced from the use of these ionisers.

Ionisers are also very efficient air cleaners – in cars as well as in our homes – removing even the tiniest particles of dust, smoke and pollen by making them fall from the air. They also remove and destroy airborne viruses and bacteria. This is why they are often referred to as Air Purifying Ionisers. The best also increase negative ions. Here are some of the claimed benefits using Ionisers, although remember that proponents may overestimate their health benefits.

- Increase your sense of well-being and mental clarity.
- Clear the air of dust, pollen, pet dander, mould spores and other potential allergens.
- Significantly decrease airborne viruses and bacteria in your home.
- Reduced instances of respiratory illnesses like colds and flu, even hay fever and asthma.
- Normalise your breathing rate, decrease blood pressure and relieve tension.
- Effective at treating Seasonal Affective Disorder (SAD).
- Improved energy levels and focus and better sleep.
- Reduces instances of headaches and sickness.
- Elevates mental concentration and performance.

Salt Lamps

These can reduce 'electric smog' in the home as they are a natural air ioniser and made from natural Himalayan crystal salt rock, formed millions of years ago in the foothills of the Himalayan mountains. They are very pleasant to look at, emitting a gentle orange glow. When placed in a room their range is limited so they are best placed near to electrical charge emitting equipment such as a TV's or Computers, to maximise their benefit. There is a theory that the much-debated sick building syndrome is also due to a build-up of positive ions from electronic equipment.

Infrared Saunas

Infrared saunas detox the millions of sweat glands covering the body which are infused with fluid from the blood. In turn, they empty on to the skin's surface, thereby flushing large amounts of toxins, including toxic acids and heavy metals, from the body.

Throughout the world, different forms of saunas are being used, from sweat lodges, practised regularly by Native American Indians, and many other indigenous cultures, to steam Saunas and Infrared Saunas.

One particular type of Sauna, that is seen to be the most beneficial, is the Near Infrared Sauna, which is the same type of infrared heat as that produced by the sun and required by all living things to gain optimum health.

The regular use of saunas helps to remove impurities from your cells, specifically the cells inside our fat, where our body stores waste and harmful toxins such as heavy metals. There is now no question that accumulated toxins are behind nearly every disease, symptom, injury and malfunction of the body.

Near Infrared Saunas use about 1/3 less electricity to operate than the Far Infrared Saunas. In addition it must be noted that "ALL Far Infrared-Saunas emit very harmful electromagnetic waves and is one real reason to avoid them" Dr Lawrence Wilson[95].

Saunas are used and loved by health professionals, athletes and celebrities around the world, many people use this infrared therapy to help them live longer, healthier and pain free lives, lose weight, relax, relieve unwanted pain, increase blood circulation and purify the skin. Sweating is one of the body's most natural ways to eliminate toxins, making it a crucial part of detoxification. Dr William L Marcus[96] supports this method and Dr Robert O. Young[97] cited in "Detoxification through the skin" advocates this for home use and in Veterinary Medicine. Whilst each type of sauna has its beneficial effects, the Near Infrared Sauna is today considered to be the most cost effective, the safest, easiest to use and the least toxic to the body.

Dr Haller[98] from Germany, in supporting the use of saunas says "If we would stop using fever suppressing medicine we would see a lot more healthy people and our natural way to fight infections would still work. Raised body temperatures of 102°F/38.9°C are considered very common and are extremely healthy".

There are reports that the claims made about the benefits of saunas are not credible. We need to make up our own minds on the information available.

Hair Tissue Mineral Analysis (HTMA)

One way to find the level of one's own body's trace mineral content is to have a Hair Analysis test. This is an accurate laboratory-screening test which can identify and measure the mineral content and a wide range of toxic trace elements, through the analysis of your hair sample. This is a useful, reliable and inexpensive screening. (See Hair Mineral State[99]).

Airnergy

I am introducing this to you, as it has such a comprehensive health enhancing and preventative affect. It is a portable, compact medical device for use in the home that creates "energised air" that feeds every cell in your body with oxygen. Spirovital Airnergy[100].

This energised oxygen promotes the creation of anti-oxidative enzymes at cell level, reducing the production of harmful free radicals and optimising the body's own immune system. It also maintains and maximises health, as the ageing process kicks in.

Research shows it has extensive benefits to our health. Dr Chris Steele[101]. It can be used for all ages to help the regular functionality of all vital functions such as breathing, heart activity, blood pressure, metabolism and hormone balance and in the prevention of macular degeneration. Best benefit of use is 20 mins per day, breathing in this energised air.

PolarAid Health Disc[102]

"If you want to find the secrets of the universe, think in terms of energy, frequency and vibration." Nikola Tesla[103] the inventor of the Tesla coil and alternating current machinery. He used science to prove that humans are energy. George Lakhovsky[104], a Russian engineer, took the work of Nikola Tesla and developed a large device which harnessed the vibrational energy around us.

Dr Dino Tomic[105], a medical doctor with an interest in alternative medicine, knew the principle, that when we lack vital energy, our body cells weaken and disease occurs. He set out to devise a way that we could use ourselves at home, to harness this energy. After extensive research he designed the PolarAid Health disc, which is a small disc which can be placed on different parts of the body to revitalise our energy levels allowing organs to regenerate and function. There are, as we know, obstructions in our environment today, depleting our absorption of this vital energy. This disc can help us absorb this energy efficiently.

Pulsed Electromagnetic Fields (PEMF)

Science has clarified that everything is energy. Energy is always dynamic and, therefore, has a frequency, which changes by the second or minute.

As all energy is electromagnetic in nature, all atoms, chemicals and cells produce electromagnetic fields (EMFs). Every organ in the body produces its own signature bio electromagnetic field and our bodies actually project their own magnetic fields. All 70 trillion cells in the body communicate via electromagnetic frequencies. Nothing happens in the body without an electromagnetic exchange. When the electromagnetic activity of the body ceases, life ceases.

Pulsed Electro Magnetic Field equipment consists of a metal ring to place around the body or a type of blanket which when switched on, pulses out magnetic fields which correspond to the body's own natural vibrations. It is natural and produces no side effects and no possibility of a therapy overdose. Basically there are no absolute contra-indications, apart from caution in the Treatment of Juvenile Diabetes, Pregnancy and those with a Pacemaker. Manfred Fichter[106].

Worldwide, thousands of these PEMF therapy devices (Magnetotron, Biopulse, Vitapulse, Sanapulse, Vitra) are currently in use in clinics, hospitals, physician's offices and physiotherapeutic institutes, for home use and in Veterinary Medicine.

The regular use of such machines greatly increases and normalises the haemoglobin cell walls interiorly and exteriorly so that the take up of oxygen level occurs more readily. This has the effect of re-establishing our energy levels and has a healing effect on a number of problems.

Having healthy cells is not a passive process. Active, regular tuning-up of our cells is now, not only feasible, but necessary, in order to slow aging and reduce the risk of cell dysfunction. Dr Pawluk[107]. The use of this type of machine several times a week will aid in all manner of healing. It greatly enhances the healing of fractures and also leg ulcers that usually take a long time to heal. Any sprain or joint injury is healed more quickly.

An important point here is that application of these Pulsating Electro Magnetic Fields (PEMFs) is not the same as the manmade, unnatural EMFs which come from electrical wiring and equipment and which cause the electro smog all around us. PEMF machines actually heal the damage from EMFs and help to regenerate our cells. The difference lies in the fact that PEMF are tuned into the body's own electric pulses to heal and do not therefore invade or damage.

Resperate

Similar to the quietening and focussing of the mind in meditation, this instructional device can lead to a calming effect, beneficial in maintaining a healthy Blood Pressure level. It must be practiced consistently to provide this benefit. Dr Chris Steele[108].

Scenar

The name is an acronym describing its function: Self-Controlled Energo-Neuro-Adaptive-Regulator. This is a small hand-held device – about the size of a mobile phone – which is successfully being used by physiotherapists, medical doctors, and natural health practitioners in clinics and hospitals. The basic model can also be used by patients themselves to instantly reduce pain when an injury occurs or as an extension with a therapeutic treatment series. You may feel a slight tingling sensation, as the device brushes over your skin.

The Scenar was developed as a part of a secret Soviet Space program[109]. The main goal was to create a small, portable, economical but most importantly, highly effective device, which could be used as a non-invasive regulator of bodily functions. They created a small, portable, economical but most importantly, highly effective device, which could keep the health of the astronauts in peak health when in space flight. This was so they did not have to resort to standard medicines, which was undesirable because the astronauts have to recycle their urine for drinking water. Medical chemicals would not be eliminated by this recycling and would remain in the water for all to drink.

Based on the principles of traditional Chinese medicine – acupuncture and zonal contact massage and the achievements of modern electro-therapy, the Scenar brilliantly combines the most up-to-date electronic technology with the ancient healing art of the East, and has brought the highest of state awards to its creators.

In a most natural and delicate way the Scenar helps the human body to correct and complete its self-recovery programme, stimulating the release of its own "internal pharmacy" and providing the organism with a freedom of choice of the necessary healing substances. See – How it Works[110].

It is a breakthrough in non-invasive healthcare. Practitioners and research studies show that patients can recover up to 70% faster by interacting directly with one of the main control mechanisms of the human body the neural response. No 'deep tissue massage' work is ever needed. The treatment is not invasive but gentle.

Evidence based trials show that, with the right stimuli, the human body is able to allocate more internal healing resources to speed up recovery from chronic pains, chronic diseases and injuries. Scenar technology and treatment protocols have been designed to facilitate this process and bring faster results than most other therapies. It is designed to interact directly with the nervous system to enable the body to heal itself independently from these types of complaints or injuries.

As the Scenar impulse is similar to endogenous nerve impulses, it is non-damaging and safe. Only people with cardiac pacemakers cannot be treated.

Zona Plus

Thousands now use the device – Zona Plus – to maintain healthy blood pressure.

During the 1970s, a team of scientists working for the U.S. Air Force, under the direction of cardiopulmonary physiologist Dr Ronald L Wiley[111] of the University of Miami, Ohio, was commissioned to find a solution to the problem of "G-force blackout" in fighter pilots at the controls of supersonic aircraft. It was noticed that squeezing this small, hand-held device, triggers a healthy change in blood pressure, by producing four beneficial effects on the cardiovascular system:

- Helps to improve function of the endothelium (arterial lining).
- Changes the autonomic nervous system back into balance, called a switch in vagal tone which is tied to ensuring blood vessels dilate properly, to helping the body maintain an appropriate heart rate and healthy hormone secretion from the kidneys.
- Stimulates production of nitric oxide and causes opening of blood vessels.
- Increases flexibility and reduces stiffness of the arterial system.

An electronic brain inside the Zona Plus instructs users to apply the precise amount of squeezing pressure needed for it to generate the greatest cardiovascular benefits. It is the only FDA cleared medical device which conveniently allows you to perform isometric exercise in the comfort of your home. Isometric exercise is where muscles in the body are given a workout, but without the strain on the joints or bones that aerobic exercise or weight training require.

Ways to Minimise Radiation Sources

We cannot stop radiation but we can help to protect us from these emissions. Bio protective systems are able to neutralise harmful EMF by neutralising their effect.

Earthing

Most people, even in this scientific age, are unaware of their bio-electrical nature and the energetic connection between our bodies and the earth. We do not now walk around in our bare feet and we sleep on beds made from insulating material so we are disconnected from the Earth's surface and its healing benefits. Mother Earth constantly sends out "vibes" which can keep us healthy and also heal us. Scientists are just now beginning to realise that by being disconnected from these natural waves of energy, we are prone to dysfunction, inflammation-related diseases and accelerated aging. We have lost our natural electrical healing roots. Clinton Ober[112].

When we connect to the earth, our body's natural internal electrical stability and rhythms are restored, which then promotes normal functioning of the body, including the cardiovascular, respiratory, digestive and immune systems.

We are children of the universe and need to be connected to our Mother Earth to remain healthy. "Illnesses do not come upon us out of the blue. They are developed from small daily sins against Nature. When enough sins have accumulated, illness will suddenly appear". Hippocrates.

The Earth is an electrical planet and we are bioelectrical beings living on this electrical planet. Our body functions electrically, our heart and nervous system are prime examples. So, when we connect to the earth, our body's natural internal electrical stability and rhythms are restored, which then promote normal functioning of the body, including the cardio-vascular, respiratory, digestive and immune systems.

Our immune system has evolved over many years. In the beginning we walked barefoot and were connected to the earth. Now being disconnected through walking on concrete roads and living in houses, built on concrete, it appears that our immune system is not being given the support of the Earth's natural electricity and is unable to deal with inflammation – the underlying cause of so many chronic illnesses. Our health stands to benefit in multiple ways, when we reconnect to the natural frequencies of the environment, but deprived of this, we more readily succumb to inflammation. All chronic disease stems from being in an inflammatory state.

Ways we can re-connect to the earth: walk barefoot where possible and in the summer wear grounding Flip Flops. Grounding shoes and boots are also available for everyday wear. Sleep on a 'grounding' or 'earthing' sheet. (Clint Ober and Roy Riggs[113]).

Geopathic Stress

This can be reversed remotely and permanently, without expensive devices! Jeff Jeffries[114].

WiFi

Geobiologist and EMF expert, Roy Riggs BSc[115] shares the dangers of electromagnetic fields and explores the key steps you can take to reduce your exposure and improve your health.

You don't need Wi-Fi in the home, school or office. A far more efficient and environmentally friendly set-up would be to buy a hard wired router such as a Linksys Cable/DSL Router or Netgear ADLS2 Modem Router with 4 port 10/100 Mbps Switch (DG834) together with a dlan High speed Ethernet Installation starter kit from www.devolo.com. This will enable you to route the internet signal through your house ring circuit enabling you to use as many computers as you want from any room with full internet connection without the Wi-Fi.

Sounds complicated but is surprisingly inexpensive simple to set up and use.

If you go to Roy Riggs website (www.royriggsuk) and click on Baby Monitors on his home page you will find a couple of recommendations as to where you can still get non digital baby alarms, which do the same thing without the microwaves.

Bedside clocks usually have the transformers inside the clock housing. Most others are usually black and look like big 3 point plugs and are hot to touch. Make sure all transformers are at least two feet away from your body.

TV and computer screens – best to change your old cathode-ray monitors (the ones with the deep backs) to any type of flat screen monitor as these give off far fewer electromagnetic fields than the old type, which thankfully you can't buy any more.

Main ring & lighting circuits – Your body voltage is highest where you sleep. Naturally your body voltage should be in harmony and in equilibrium with the earth's natural Schumann-based electrical field, which is under 350 mV and normally stable at about 2 mV. The average person sleeps with a body voltage of about 2,500 mV or more. Unplug your WiFi System at night and sleep on an 'earthing sheet' to reduce the voltage. (Roy Riggs).

Following all the above advice, will make an immense difference to you and your family's health. (See also Clinton Ober et al on these matters).

Q-link

A Q-Link is a pendant worn around the neck at the centre of your chest and is said to support the body's own natural frequencies. The resulting resonant effect is similar to the healthy, energizing experiences we have in nature, allowing us to have positive interactions with others, while participating in self-balancing, restorative activities. Because it takes less effort and energy to maintain an object already functioning at more ideal 'resonance frequencies', the more often you wear or use Q-Link, the better it can work for you.

It doesn't matter whether you wear it inside or outside a shirt or blouse. Your Q-Link begins to create a linked energy system over time – a sympathetic resonance effect, to use the technical term. This effect reinforces and enhances specific life-supporting energies in your bio field.

The Q-Link may, among other benefits, increase physical stamina, reduces stress, increases ability to focus and can also reduce the effect of jet lag. It has been designed to help the body protect itself from the environmental stresses of EMFs.

With a Q-Link, the recharging of your bio field is happening whenever you wear it. So it is advantageous to wear it all the time, even when you sleep. It is especially valuable when you are exposed to strong

Electromagnetic Fields, such as in front of a computer monitor, while on a cell phone, or if you live near high-voltage power lines. (See – Meaningful Health[116]).

Blushield products[117]

These are active ways to protect ourselves and to minimise EMF which can be used for the Home, School Office and Travel.

Earthcalm[118]

The results of research on this device, clearly indicates that the harmful effect of different Electro Magnetic environments is completely reversed when the Infinity device is plugged into a home wall socket.

See Lloyd Burrell[119], who has a range of devices that will help us and our children, live a naturally healthy life, in our electromagnetic world.

In conclusion, the above are some of the known ways available, to protect ourselves, from the all-pervading electro smog surrounding us and the very real dangers, that are now known, to be detrimental to our health. They are not necessarily the only systems available so the reader is urged to research further[120].

We will now enter the world of the many trained and qualified healing practitioners...

I hope that the days come easy and the moments pass slow,
And each road leads you where you want to go,
And if you're faced with a choice, and you have to choose,
I hope you choose the one that means the most to you.
And if one door opens to another door closed,
I hope you keep on walkin' till you find the window,
If it's cold outside, show the world the warmth of your smile,
But more than anything, more than anything,
My wish, for you, is that this life becomes all that you want it to,
Your dreams stay big, and your worries stay small,
You never need to carry more than you can hold,
And while you're out there getting where you're getting to,
I hope you know somebody loves you,
...and wants the same things too,
Yeah, this is my wish.

"My Wish" by Rascal Flats

> "A good teacher is like a candle — it consumes itself to light the way for others."
> ~ Mustafa Kemal Ataturk

Part 8: Classes Promoting Health with Qualified Practitioners

For those of you who would like to know how our health can be enhanced by other means, I present a few ways that are taught in classes, run by qualified teachers.

Tai Qi

Tai Qi (pronounced Tie Chee) is a Chinese Martial Art and is seen as the life energy or vital energy well understood by the Chinese. The idea is that Qi is a fundamental concept in Chinese medicine being the vital force that activates every function and drives every process in the human body. It can be compared to an electric current. Qi, by the way, is also the energy stimulated by Acupuncture treatments.

There are several types of Tai Qi. The one that is seen to be of the greatest benefit to health is Qi Gong (often spelt Chi Kung) a powerful type of health exercise, which has been practised for centuries by millions of Chinese people. It is based on repetitions of very precise sets of movements, specifically designed to benefit health on many different levels.

Qi Gong is easy to learn and enjoyable to do. Even a few minutes of practise can have an invigorating and rejuvenating effect. Regular practice brings about a deep strengthening effect for the whole body and its various systems (nervous, digestive, respiratory, skeletal, muscular, hormonal and gynaecological). Its ability to help in healing a large variety of chronic and acute injuries and illnesses has been the subject of various research programmes led by Chinese medical authorities.

The movement of Qi (energy) in the body is enhanced by opening certain gates and stretching and twisting energy channels. A further key point in Qi Gong practice is relaxation and deep breathing, both of which are prerequisites allowing Qi to flow.

With a little bit of regular practice, Qi Gong can have a powerful effect on mind, body and spirit. Reported benefits have included increased general health and well-being, reduced levels of stress, and a brighter and more balanced outlook on life's possibilities.

Other healing benefits of medical Qi Gong are that it enhances brain function and so is a great aid in preventing the onset of senility. Overall and more importantly it enhances the immune system, our own means of preventing disease. A most enjoyable way to enhance health.

Yoga

Yoga is a Hindu spiritual and ascetic discipline, a part of which includes breath control, simple meditation, and the adoption of specific bodily postures. It is widely practised for health and relaxation and is a simple process of reversing the ordinary outward flow of energy and consciousness so that the mind becomes a dynamic centre of direct perception no longer dependent upon the fallible senses but capable of actually experiencing Truth.

The word yoga itself means "union" of the individual consciousness or soul with the Universal Consciousness or Spirit. Though many people think of yoga only as physical exercises – the Asana's or postures have gained widespread popularity in recent decades – these are really only the most superficial aspect of this profound science which can unfold the infinite potentials of the human mind and soul.

Ordinarily our awareness and energies are directed outward, to the things of this world, which we perceive through the limited instruments of our five senses. Because human reason has to rely upon the partial and often deceptive data supplied by the physical senses, we must learn to tap deeper and to more subtle levels of awareness, if we are to solve the enigmas of life – Who am I? Why am I here? How do I realize Truth?

Research makes it clear that yoga deserves a permanent place at the health and fitness table, alongside other forms of exercise that may be more familiar to most people. To put it another way, if you like yoga, don't feel like you're missing out if you're not also putting in time on the treadmill or exercise bike. "Yoga seems to be able to provide many of the physical benefits of exercise – and more. It behaves as both exercise and meditation" Adam Bean[121].

The stretching, compressing and twisting of the gut with Yoga exercises also enhances and supports of the digestive system. WDDTY Nov 2015[122].

In 2010, researchers at the University Of Maryland School Of Nursing[123] published a comparative analysis of 81 studies that examined yoga's health benefits and the health benefits of aerobic exercise. The researchers found yoga to be especially effective at reducing stress by lowering cortisol, the stress hormone. This may not be news to those who practise yoga, but even die-hard enthusiasts will be surprised at the number of other health benefits yoga can confer – often to a larger degree than aerobic exercise. The researchers found that yoga outperformed aerobic exercise at improving balance, flexibility, strength, pain levels among seniors, menopausal symptoms, daily energy level, and social and occupation functioning, among other health parameters. J Altern[124].

In addition the regular practice of Yoga also prevents muscle deterioration, bone weakness and also prevent cartilage and joint breakdown. By improving blood flow, it aids in preventing stagnation of the arterial and lymphatic system, the physical consequences associated with this lack of flow. This will happen when these two systems are not supported, since they both play a vital part in the maintenance of our health and in the prevention of disease. Dana Blinder[125].

Pilates

Joseph Pilates[126] developed these exercises in the 1920s, as a way to help injured athletes and dancers safely return to exercise and maintain their fitness. Since then, Pilates has been adapted to suit people in the general community.

They consist of low-impact flexibility, muscular strength and endurance movements emphasizing proper postural alignment, core strength and muscle balance. In Pilates the chance of injury is much lower than with other more strenuous forms of exercise. Pilates also focuses on the mind-body connection. While doing the various exercises your mind needs to be constantly aware of your breathing and the way your body moves.

It is a safe and effective method of rehabilitation and exercise focussing on muscular balance. The health benefits include: improved flexibility, increased muscle strength and tone – particularly of your abdominal muscles, lower back, hips and buttocks – the core muscles of your body, by balancing muscular strength on both sides of your body. It is an aid to stress management and relaxation.

N/B For all of the above it is worthwhile to seek medical advice before embarking on any program, should you have any concerns.

Help is available to be healthy. Knowing what this is and how to obtain it is key. The following pages will give you an overview...

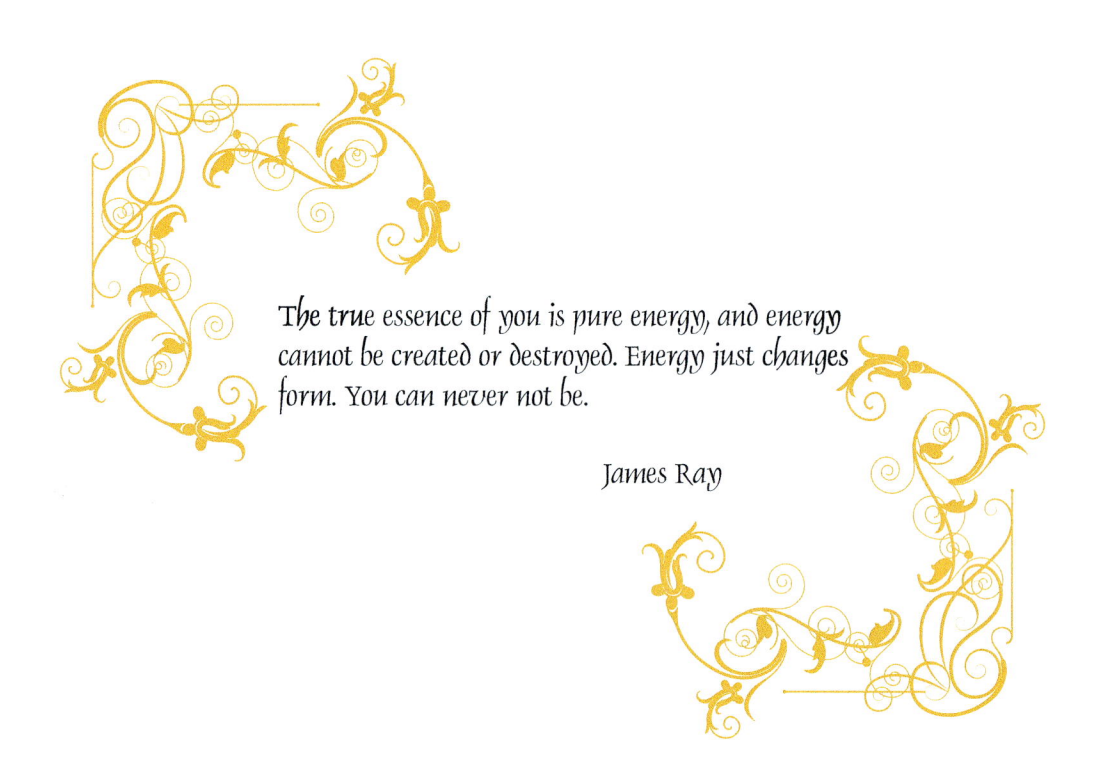

The true essence of you is pure energy, and energy cannot be created or destroyed. Energy just changes form. You can never not be.

James Ray

Part 9: Health Maintenance with trained Practitioners

There is an abundance of ways that trained practitioners, other than those in the medical profession, can prevent and heal illness. When qualified, these practitioners use their skill and treat patients according to the accepted standards of their profession, they will do no harm. As in all professions there are variations in how treatment is carried out.

The field of complementary therapies is diverse. Explained here are some that are most commonly understood, and I have included the main benefits of each. It is an introduction to the wide and varied world of natural therapies and will hopefully help you choose an appropriate treatment for your circumstances.

Acupuncture

Acupuncture is a holistic health technique that stems from Traditional Chinese Medicine. Contrary to popular Western belief, acupuncture is not just a system for inserting very fine needles into specific body locations to alleviate pain, it is a complete medical protocol focused on correcting imbalances of energy in the body to help or treat various conditions. From its inception in China more than 2,500 years ago, acupuncture has been used traditionally to prevent, diagnose and treat disease, as well as to improve general health and today acupuncture is one of the most popular practices of Traditional Chinese Medicine (TCM).

Studies show that acupuncture can and does stimulate the body's natural functions to heal and regulate a great many conditions by stimulating the endogenous opioid peptides in the central nervous system, as these play an essential role in mediating the analgesic effect and reducing pain. (Neuroscience Letters[127]).

Acupressure

Acupressure is similar in practice to acupuncture, only that no needles are involved. Practitioners use their hands, elbows, or feet to apply pressure to specific points along the body's "meridians." According to the theory behind acupressure[128], meridians are channels that carry life energy (qi or ch'i) throughout the body. The reasoning holds that illness can occur when one of these meridians is blocked or out of balance; acupressure is thought to relieve blockages so energy can flow freely again, restoring wellness. More research is needed, but pilot studies have found positive results: Acupressure might decrease nausea for chemotherapy patients and reduce anxiety in people scheduled to have surgery.

Alexander Technique

Much of the early medical research on the Alexander Technique was conducted during the 1940s by Dr Wilfred Barlow MD[129], a Consultant Rheumatologist at Guy's Hospital in London, England. The Alexander Technique is a skill for self-development, teaching you to change long-standing habits that cause unnecessary tension in everything you do. It is a way to feel better, and to move in a more relaxed and comfortable way, the way nature intended.

An Alexander Technique teacher helps you to identify and lose the harmful habits you have built up over a lifetime. Whatever your age or ability, the Technique can help boost your performance in any activity and relieve the pain and stress caused by bad postural habits, like slouching or rounded shoulders.

Everyday things, like tensing when the phone rings, rushing to pick up the children from school, or worrying about deadlines, all can lead to physical and mental strain. Over the years, this tension accumulates and can result in illness, injury or common aches and pains that seem to come from nowhere.

Working with your teacher, you will learn to recognise your usual reactions to the stresses of life. You will find out how you have been contributing to your problems, how to prevent them and regain control – a method of re-education.

Alexander Technique lessons stimulate your ability to learn simultaneously on different levels; physically, intellectually and emotionally. You learn to recognise your harmful habits, how to stop and think, and to choose a better response. Gradually you learn to apply your new understanding and skill in everyday activities and more complex ones, to bring awareness and poise into everything you do. Just like riding a bike, once learned, the technique stays with you for life!

Ayurvedic Medicine

Ayurvedic medicine (also called Ayurveda) is one of the world's oldest medical systems. It originated in India more than 3,000 years ago and remains one of the country's traditional health care systems.

This type of medicine is based on scientific observations and offers a rudimentary but rational system for interpretation of the body, its vital functions and its diseases, by using a holistic approach incorporating all physical and psychological manifestations. According to the ancient Indian concept the Universe is composed of 5 elements – emptiness, wind, fire, water and earth. Considerations of these elements are important in determining treatment as is the persons own psyche. Over time this medicine has used three thousand plant species of which one thousand are still in use. Where such medications are used, it is important to investigate the current known effects of these in all circumstances.

Of all the ancient medical traditions Ayurveda has always paid the greatest attention to hygiene, diet and to preventive and curative medicine. These traditional rules are set out in the ancient Sanskrit medical treaties and are adhered to by the practitioner. This tradition of personal hygiene and bathing is considered to be of great importance as this activity is seen to aid in a number of ailments including clarifying the blood and stimulating the digestion.

Bioenergetics

Bioenergetics is a body movement technique with a difference. The various body positions are specifically designed to release 'holding patterns' from the skin and muscle system of the body (the fascia). Thus Bioenergetics, whilst on the surface resembling Yoga, Pilates, or a gym workout, it is actually radically different. It is a form of body Psychotherapy that is used to allow the human being to achieve their potential in all aspects of their lives.

Bioenergetic screening can suggest possible functional/subclinical imbalances in the body, based on distortions in the body-field. This makes it an excellent complement to medical screening.

The creation of Bioenergetics is generally credited to Alexander Lowen 1910–2008[130], an American psychotherapist who was originally a student of Wilhelm Rech[131] – himself a student of Carl Jung[132]. However, different schools of Bioenergetics have arisen over the years, with different exercises and different general approaches arising with them. It's fair to say that no single coherent source for Bioenergetics exists.

The trained therapist reads the body, resonates with its energy, feels the emotions, and identifies chronic muscular tensions held in the body. Tensions are the result of difficulties experienced in our lives and will be evident to the practitioner. 'Holding positions' will be recommended to enable their release.

Managing these effects on our bodies can lead onto expanding the capacity for intimacy, healing sexual difficulties and learning new, more fulfilling ways of relating to others. Tenderness, aggression, assertion – and their confluence in sexuality – are seen as core lifesaving forces and all reflect in the body posture. The therapeutic relationship provides a place of safety in which healing begins. Routine exercises will be given so that each person can then practise for themselves. (See Video explanation[133]).

Bioresonance/MORA Therapy

The Mora therapy – known as bioresonance therapy, is a holistic diagnostic and treatment principle, working with a person's energy oscillations. This therapy model was developed in 1977 by the German duo of Dr. Franz Morell and engineer Erich Rasche[134], hence the name MO-RA.

Mora therapy is a complete assessment and treatment device. The client holds two brass cathodes in each hand and places their feet on a brass plate. Our body has energy points on all our fingers and toes, representing different organs. The practitioner accesses these energy points, with a stylus – also connected to the machine. The energy levels for all organs are then recorded by the machine so that a full organ reading is taken. These energy levels are then fed back into the client as a treatment, to balance the clients own body energy. The only energy ever used, is the client's own.

Years of research by renowned scientists have determined and verified that every human being has an individual oscillation spectrum that can be used therapeutically. Today, it is also a known fact that physiological activities in the bodies of human beings and animals can be controlled using electromagnetic oscillations. Even the organs, be they healthy or diseased, have an entirely individual oscillation spectrum that varies from person to person.

The underlying theory behind this is that every cell in the body resonates at a particular frequency. This takes the form of an electro-magnetic field and groups of cells in an organ or system have multiple frequency patterns which are unique. Hence, the whole body has a unique complex frequency make up which can change or become distorted when affected by illness.

If you accept that our cells are controlled by our own natural electro-magnetic field, then it logical to introduce healthy frequencies to re-balance the whole body and provide an environment where the body cures itself. This treatment therefore appears to have connections with the principles of acupuncture and homeopathy which rely on energy flow and the imprinting of frequencies in aqueous solutions.

The MORA therapy uses endogenic oscillations that correspond to the current physiological condition of the patient. Once this information is electronically processed and fed back, it is possible to change the physical and physiological conditions in the body of a patient and to initiate healing processes specifically.

This therapy is neither an electric therapy nor radiation in any form and it is also not a method where one needs to have faith in order to see visible results. It is based on over 30 years of experience and has also been substantiated by scientific research to some extent. The MORA therapy concept has also been corroborated by modern research in the field of bio electromagnetism.

This machine can measure the level of energy flowing through each organ and it will then show which organs are inflammatory (too much) and which are degenerative (too little). The clients own energies will then be returned to them in treatment mode. This method counteracts any previous fluctuations of energy, and creates a healthy balance in all organs.

Indications of depleted energy in organs – which are potential sources of disease – can then be rectified, many weeks/months prior to any disease symptoms appearing. This balancing is essential for the health of all organs.

This is a non-invasive treatment in the hands of a trained therapist, with no known adverse side effects, as it is using the persons own energy oscillations to feedback and then rectify.

In Summary, MORA therapy improves the immune system/improves hormonal response/cleanses the connective tissue and slows down the ageing process of organs and tissues. Today, there are over 8000 BICOM devices in Germany, (17,000 worldwide in 80 countries) used by both medical practitioners in private practice and by complementary therapists. Bioresonance therapy is widely used in other countries such as Austria and Switzerland and also in the Netherlands, and there are a few therapists in the UK. It is starting to become more well-known outside Europe, especially in China, where BICOM devices are used in government hospitals, primarily children's hospitals. In other countries, including Australia, bioresonance is seen as a complementary therapy. There are some who still remain doubtful as to its effectiveness, as is the case with many claims about methods used in any alternative field, even despite sound scientific knowledge regarding the basis of these treatments.

Bowen Technique

Bowen therapy, or the Bowen technique, is a non-invasive, complementary therapy. It targets certain points on the body with gentle rolling movements to help it balance, repair and reset itself.

Developed in the 1950s by Tom Bowen[135], this therapy is reported to help with a number of conditions and can also address symptoms of stress and anxiety. It is important to note that Bowen therapy focuses on the whole person, not just the condition. The Bowen therapist will know a number of movements that affect certain areas of the body. How does Bowen therapy work?

As humans, we have the ability to develop responses to stimuli extremely quickly. For instance, if we find ourselves in danger we quickly determine how to respond to it. The same goes for all other situations. A Bowen therapist will use pressure that is appropriate for the individual, so the movements do not provoke the body's natural defence system. Therefore, Bowen therapy gives our bodies a much needed break in the treatment, during which they are able to reset.

There are many theories as to how Bowen treatment actually works. Many questions are raised as to how it helps to prompt muscles and tissue in the body to repair and heal. Although research is still ongoing, many theories conclude that it has something to do with how the brain reacts to neural stimulus. The changes to behaviour demonstrated that Bowen therapy affects more than isolated muscles and connective tissue.

The brain emits around 600,000 signals per second. These send out signals and in turn receive information from the body. For example, a muscular movement begins from the front part of the brain and is sent via signals through the spinal cord, to a part of the body where it transforms into movement. In order to send this muscle movement signal, however, the brain must first receive a signal telling it what is happening and why this muscle must be moved. This sending and receiving of information operates in a loop circuit, with signals travelling at fast speeds.

Bowen therapy fits into this theory because of how the rolling movements — and the regular intervals between each sequence — interfere with signals to the brain. This creates another set of variables for the brain to examine. Once the brain begins to reorder the signals it is also able to receive and interpret information coming from other areas of the body. This explains why Bowen therapy is able to treat ailments that a patient may not have been aware of. By interfering with the brain's controlled loop circuit of signals, Bowen therapy helps the brain to pinpoint other areas in the body that may need healing and repairing.

Tom Bowen was a very observational person. He could see when parts of the body were subtly imbalanced, so he could then begin treatment quickly. After making a movement in a therapy session, he would leave the room for a few minutes, before returning to check how the patient's body had responded. This would determine if anything else needed to be done.

The principle of resting the body for a couple of minutes is vital as it starts the process of repair. The length of time between procedures will differ from client to client. The breaks, however, can be hard to master as they are one of the least understood and most difficult principles to learn as a Bowen therapist. They are considered the most important element, to allow the time needed for the repair to begin.

As this technique is so effective, it has been widely embraced by a broad spectrum of people. Health professionals are impressed by the effectiveness of the Bowen technique and the diversity of problems addressed by it and its efficacy in preventing further imbalances.

Chelation Therapy.

Chelation therapy is the intravenous use of EDTA (ethylene diamine tetra acetic acid) given to bind toxic heavy metals, as well as to bind calcium in areas of the body where it is harmful and causing problems. EDTA also binds trace minerals. These bound molecules are then excreted via the kidneys through the urine. EDTA is a synthetic amino acid and is one of many different substances used as a chelating agent.

Chelation therapy is a dynamic therapy as mentioned above, that has at least two major effects. As mentioned above, it can remove heavy toxic metals such as arsenic, lead and mercury and most importantly, EDTA improves arterial circulation and so addresses the number-one cause of death of heart disease, and stroke, which is not far behind. Other diseases including eye disorders and diabetes, such as macular degeneration and glaucoma, also have associated circulatory problems and EDTA is the only therapy we have, that can address these. It is a powerful therapy that should have a huge impact on extending and improving the quality of life in people as they get older – a beautiful longevity medicine. Terry

Chappell[136] practises integrated medicine which combines the best of conventional and alternative medicine.

NHS Doctors have used the molecule for decades to treat heavy metal poisoning. In those cases it is given intravenously. EDTA is also an ingredient in some prescription cancer-fighting medicines. It is also used as an emergency treatment for hypercalcaemia (excessive calcium levels) and the control of ventricular arrhythmias (abnormal heart rhythms) associated with digitalis toxicity[137].

The American Medical Association[138], while not yet endorsing chelation therapy for arteriosclerosis, does approve its use in the treatment of lead and other heavy metal poisoning.

People who use chelation therapy are generally those who already have heart disease or wish to implement preventative measures, especially if there is a family history of heart disease. Chelation is also found to be beneficial in the treatment of other conditions such as osteoarthritis, chronic fatigue syndrome, fibromyalgia and organic poisoning. There are very few medical procedures that can report, as can chelation, no fatalities. Although used by the medical profession in some cases, chelation therapy is not generally available.

Every year, in contrast, prescribed drugs, hospital accidents and mistakes result in many deaths. Modern medicine now has the benefit of a long history of chelation having been used for many conditions. Those who specialize in it are sure of these benefits, and the very best ways of using it.

Following the guidelines of the American College of Advancement of Medicine (ACAM) [139], estimates are that at least 500,000 patients have received over 10,000,000 chelation treatments without a single fatality being attributed to it. This cannot be said about surgical procedures. However it is not a treatment that is offered in the NHS and generally medical doctors are not in favour. Interestingly Germany and Australia approve of chelation and it is widely practised there. There are several private centres in the UK that specialise in this treatment.

EDTA chelation may be one of the most effective, least expensive, and safest treatments for heart disease, ever developed.

Chiropractic and Osteopathy

A chiropractor is a regulated healthcare professional who focuses on the relationship between your body's structure – largely the spine – and how it functions.

Chiropractic is a healthcare discipline that emphasizes the inherent recuperative power of the body to heal itself without the use of drugs or surgery. The practise of chiropractic focuses on the relationship between structure (primarily the spine) and function (as coordinated by the nervous system) and how that relationship affects the preservation and restoration of health. In addition, doctors of chiropractic recognize the value and responsibility of working in cooperation with other health care practitioners when in the best interest of the patient. It is seen as complimentary to medical doctors to get people pain free and prevent future injuries. Dr John Bergman[140].

Chiropractors use hands-on spinal manipulation and other alternative treatments, the theory being that proper alignment of the body's musculo-skeletal structure, particularly the spine, will enable the body to heal itself without surgery or medication. If you frequently suffer with symptoms like joint pain, backaches or headaches, but are yet to ever visit a chiropractor for help, then you may be missing out on an effective and natural treatment option. Millions of people around the world have experienced the incredible benefits of chiropractic care, a holistic, non-invasive treatment approach that has been shown to help treat dozens of different conditions. One of the best things about receiving chiropractic adjustments is that they are a completely drug-free path to healing the body naturally.

There are 1080 chiropractors in the UK today, and almost one-third of these are McTimoney chiropractors – a particular branch of the profession in the UK which has developed for some years, outside of the apparent mainstream.

The McTimoney method[141] is distinguished by its gentle, whole body approach. It aims to correct the alignment of the bones of the spine and other joints of the body, to restore nerve function, to alleviate pain, and to promote natural health. The technique is suitable for the very young as well as the old and frail.

What is the difference between Osteopathy and Chiropractic?

Osteopathy is a way of detecting, treating and preventing health problems by moving, stretching and massaging a person's muscles and joints. An osteopath aims to restore the normal function and stability of the joints to help the body heal itself. They use their hands to treat your body in a variety of ways, using a mixture of gentle and forceful techniques.

Osteopathy is based on the principle that the wellbeing of an individual depends on their bones, muscles, ligaments and connective tissue functioning smoothly together. They use a range of techniques but not drugs or surgery.

In the UK, osteopathy is a complementary or alternative medicine (CAM) as it is different from conventional western medicine[142].

Osteopathy and chiropractic share a common philosophy about the importance of the integrity of the spine in ensuring good health. In fact, this philosophy is shared by almost all traditional healing arts as well as martial arts, including Yoga, Tai qi (Tai Chi), Aikido and many others. It is also found in many treatment modalities in modern complementary and alternative medicine, including structural integration or Rolfing, and the Alexander Technique.

The major difference between an Osteopath and a chiropractor is that while the chiropractor is primarily focused on the spine and joints (and the muscles too, to a point), an Osteopath is concerned with including the rest of the body. Osteopaths typically take a broader approach and may treat a larger area. Chiropractic and Osteopathy are regulated in the same way that medicine is.

Epigenetics

Much work has been done within the scientific community to establish the primary cause of disease which arises through environmental challenges that our bodies are faced with. This field of science is called Epigenetics.

It is a branch of science that is relatively new. Research began in earnest in the mid-nineties, and has only found traction in the wider scientific community in the last decade or so. The aim of the study and practice of Epigenetics is to deliver health solutions at the very core of our being.

According to some scientists, changing your health may be as 'simple' as changing your thoughts and beliefs. "Contrary to what many people are being led to believe, a lot of emphasis placed on genes determining human behaviour is nothing but theory and doctrine," writes Konstantin Erikseni[143] "We are free to make decisions that impact our lives and those of others... Our beliefs can change our biology. We have the power to heal ourselves, increase our feelings of self-worth and improve our emotional state." In a broad sense, Epigenetics is a bridge between genotype and phenotype – a phenomenon that changes the final outcome of a locus or chromosome without changing the underlying DNA sequence. There are four fundamental types of bases that comprise DNA – adenine, cytosine, guanine, and thymine amounting to approximately 3 billion of these nucleotide bases. These determine our body's instructions on how to provide important proteins – complex molecules that trigger various biological actions to carry out life functions. We are, as you can see, made up of our own and varying molecules each derived from either one of our parents and passed down through generations in the DNA – Science Direct[144].

The study of Epigenetics is the study of biological mechanisms that will switch genes on and off. What does that mean? Genetics essentially seeks to understand what affects our genes and how they are read by cells, and subsequently how they produce proteins. Epigenetics is everywhere – what you eat, where you live, who you interact with, when you sleep, how you exercise, even aging – and all of these can eventually cause chemical modifications around the genes that will turn those genes on or off over time. Additionally, in certain diseases such as cancer or Alzheimer's, various genes will be switched into the opposite state, away from the normal/healthy state.

Theoretically Epigenetics seeks to map every single cause and effect of the different combinations, and if by this, a gene's state could be reversed, by keeping the good while eliminating the bad, then we could theoretically cure cancer, slow aging, stop obesity, and so much more. Cellular biologist Bruce Lipton, PhD[145]., is one of the leading authorities on how emotions can regulate genetic expression, which are explained in-depth in his excellent books: "The Biology of Belief, and Spontaneous Evolution". "Your Emotions Regulate Your Genetic Expression".

Homeopathy

Homeopathy was discovered by a German doctor, Samuel Hahnemann[146] and first appeared in print in 1807. Hahnemann was looking for a way to reduce the damaging side effects associated with the medical treatments of his day, which included the use of poisons. He began experimenting on himself and a group of healthy volunteers, giving smaller and smaller medicinal doses, discovering that as well as reducing toxicity, the medicines became more effective as the doses were lowered.

Hahnemann came to believe that all effective drugs produce symptoms in healthy individuals similar to those of the diseases that they treat, in accord with the 'law of similars' that had been proposed by ancient physicians.

What is Homeopathic Medicine? It is a holistic medicine which uses specially prepared, highly diluted substances (given mainly in tablet form) with the aim of triggering the body's own healing mechanisms[147]. Homeopathic medicine is cheap to produce, is effective and has no known side-effects unlike conventional medicine, which is extremely expensive to research and develop and which when produced, comes in most cases, with side-effects, some of them life threatening in themselves. It is known as a complementary or alternative medicine (CAM) [148]. This means that homeopathy is different in important ways from treatments that are part of conventional Western medicine and is used to 'treat' an extremely wide range of conditions, including physical conditions such as asthma and psychological conditions such as depression.

The central principle of the 'treatment' is that 'like cures like' and that a substance that causes certain symptoms can also help to remove those symptoms. This is the basis for all homeopathic treatments. A second central principle is based around a process of dilution and shaking, called succussion. Homeopathy deals with the underlying cause of a symptom and seeks to improve a person's general level of health making them less likely to be ill in the future. WDDTY Feb 2016[149].

Homeopathy is usually practised privately and some homeopathic remedies are now available from pharmacies. The National Health Service does not recognise homeopathy as a scientific means to treat illnesses or diseases, but Britain's 400 GPs who currently prescribe it, are calling for it to be included, saying "The NHS needs more homeopathy". WDDTY May 2016[150].

Kinesiology

Kinesiology[151] is the scientific study of movement, addressing physiological, biomechanical, and psychological principles. Applied kinesiology (AK) is also known as muscle strength testing, and is a method of diagnosis and treatment based on the belief that various muscles are linked to particular organs and glands.

The body has within and surrounding it, an electrical network or grid, which is pure energy. Because energy runs through the muscles in your body, anything that impacts your electrical system that does not maintain or enhance your body's balance, will cause your muscles to 'short circuit' or temporarily weaken. Things that can have an impact on your electrical system are thoughts and emotions, foods, and other chemical substances.

Kinesiology uses the muscle's strengths or weaknesses, to find what events or emotions 'weaken' or 'strengthen' the body. It is simply a way to ask the body questions and get clear answers – like a telephone to the subconscious mind.

Because our subconscious mind knows everything, the practitioner can ask it yes or no questions and watch how the electrical system energy reacts to the degree of pressure being applied to either an arm or a leg. If a statement is true, the electrical system will continue to flow and the circuits remain strong. If a statement is false, the energy system will temporarily short circuit and muscles will quickly weaken. This will indicate whether the subconscious mind and body are congruent with the questions asked and so determine what emotional aspects might need to be addressed. The reactions cannot be falsified. The body knows the truth. See Research[152].

Massage

Massage dates back over 5,000 years ago, to ancient cultures that believed in its medical benefits. The first written records of massage therapy are found in China and Egypt. 2700 BCE: the first known Chinese text is called "The Yellow Emperor's Classic Book of Internal Medicine." Emperor Huangdi 2600BC[153].

Hippocrates[154] believed that massage had two primary uses: strengthening or relaxing muscles. Massage has many different techniques and people seek it for a variety of health-related purposes, including relieving pain, rehabilitating sports injuries, reducing stress, increasing relaxation, addressing anxiety and depression and to aid general wellness.

Reflexology

All organs of the body are represented by reflex points on the feet. Reflexology is an ancient therapy designed to bring the body back into healthful balance after it has lost this, due to unhealthy lifestyle practices, resulting in illness and pain. It provides preventative maintenance. The qualified practitioner will gently massage the feet and in the process be able to detect points at which an organ is blocked. Tender areas on the feet denote low energy in the representative organ and these can then be gently stimulated in order to rebalance and return the energy flow to prevent dis-ease.

This understanding stems from Eastern therapeutic practices based on the notion that illness is caused by a number of factors including those that have weakened the body's natural defences. The concept here is that we have energy centres that connect with one another throughout our bodies, called meridians. This energy flow sustains our organs and enables them to function at optimum level.

Reiki Therapy

Reiki is a Japanese technique for stress reduction and relaxation that also promotes healing. It is administered by 'laying on of hands' and is based on the idea that an unseen 'life force energy' flows through us and is what causes us to be alive. If one's 'life force energy' is low, then we are more likely to get sick or feel stress, and if it is high, we are more capable of being happy and healthy.

The word Reiki is made of two Japanese words: — Rei which means 'God's Wisdom or the Higher Power' and Ki which is 'life force energy'. So Reiki is actually 'spiritually guided life force energy.'

A treatment feels like a wonderful glowing radiance that flows through and around you. Reiki treats the whole person by including body, emotions, mind and spirit, creating many beneficial effects that include relaxation and feelings of peace, security and wellbeing. Many have reported miraculous results.

Reiki[155] is a simple, natural and safe method of spiritual healing and self-improvement that everyone can use. It has been effective in helping virtually every known illness and malady and always creates a beneficial effect. It also works in conjunction with all other medical or therapeutic techniques to relieve side effects and promote recovery.

An amazingly simple technique to learn, the ability to use Reiki is not taught in the usual sense, but is transferred to the student during a Reiki class. This ability is passed on during an 'attunement' given by a Reiki master and allows the student to tap into their own unlimited supply of 'life force energy' to work with and treat other people's health in enhancing their quality of life. Reiki classes are taught all over the country and in many parts of the world. It is a recognised complementary treatment in the NHS.

Rolfing

Rolfing is a technique that involves the manipulation of the fascia and soft tissue to create better alignment and balance in the body. Rolfing treats the soft tissue and fascia across the whole body, no matter where the source of the pain is, in an attempt to encourage the body to hold itself in a healthy way and release areas that might be causing imbalance and referred pain. It can create space around painful joints and allow the body to function naturally and without pain.

The technique, which was created by Dr Ida P. Rolf[156] in the 60s, is a more holistic treatment than is clinical physiotherapy or deep tissue massage, and it claims to offer both physical and mental benefits. Dr Rolf referred to her work as "structural integration." She designed the system as a way to deeply manipulate and reorganize connective tissue and fascia. Her aim was to relieve patterns of physical misalignment through a series of sessions, each focusing on a different part of the body, using deep pressure and breath work. The ultimate goal, along with resetting alignment patterns in the body, is to improve movement and posture, reduce stress and create an overall sense of wellbeing.

Injuries, bad posture/mechanics or pain, can cause the body to move incorrectly and become dysfunctional. Over time this imbalance can cause or exacerbate pain and old injuries can remain because the body is not able to move naturally, or it has got into the habit of moving in a way that is harmful or painful. Rolfing releases tight fascia that might be causing imbalance or inhibiting free, healthy movement.

The Zenni Method

Victor Zenni[157] a Doctor of science in Colombo, developed this system which involves activating the immune system.

The Zenni Method[158] is based on electrostimulation by currents — known as Bernard currents — to restore the natural electrical potentials in the cells to stimulate the repair processes in the internal organs, endocrine glands and nervous system, leading to the stopping of the disease through the elimination of its causes. WDDTY March 2018[159].

The patient is connected to the device and two electrodes are placed as needed. The therapy is completely painless. The current stimulates the central nervous system, which regulates the organs, including the thyroid gland, and influences the proper secretion of hormones, which can lead to self-healing of the body.

The Universal Law of Attraction is the ability to attract into our lives whatever we are focusing on.

The greatest and the most infallible law upon which the entire system of creation depend.

Charles Haanel

Part 10: Wealth and Success – We have a choice

A stressful life leads to ill health. We can overcome adversity.

We are energy. We are of this planet and are built of the same molecules as everything around us except in a different order. We are therefore the same as the trees, the plants, the earth and all the objects in our houses. Things are not solid, they are a mass of vibrating molecules. We are bound, by existing in this particular dimension, to see things as solid. If we were to experience another dimension it is possible we could then pass through walls and all around us we would experience as shimmering with no solidity. We are, as is everything around us, pure energy vibrating among other vibrating beings and objects. Those familiar with the days of the program "Star Trek" will remember the phrase "Beam me up Scotty" showing the person morphing into a vibrating mass. Well that was ahead of possibility – or was it? If our energy was harnessed we could light up a whole town. We are in truth a great part of this Universal Vibrating Intelligence.

This is an enormous concept to realise and if we are to follow on from this then we need to understand that the thoughts we have, are also energy and that they will have an end point – in other words they will make a connection. "What we think we attract" – it is an inevitability. The life that we now live, is the consequence of our past thoughts. We are absolutely responsible for our own life's journey. We attract what we think and believe in. The natural laws of the universe are precise. This wonderful revelation means we can achieve anything we want. Nothing comes to pass except through our thoughts. So it is as if our brain is like an electric station. When we think, we are activating a vibration in our bodies and a connection will be made. This knowledge will enable us to take full control of how we live our lives, as we will attract back to us that which we send out. Our thoughts will return to us from the vibrating universe in the frequency we set up. The Universe is intelligent and will deliver at a time that is right for us. An interesting feature of this phenomenon is that what we receive may not always be what we actually imagined it would be! It will however be the best for us. The world is changing and the past is not recognisable in today's developed world. What is your life right now? Your mind actually created what you now experience in all your living ways. Is that hard to understand?

> *"Whatever the mind can conceive and believe, the mind can achieve regardless of how many times you have failed in the past or how lofty your aims and hopes may be"*
>
> —Napoleon Hill[160]

Understand, the conscious mind is the goal setter, and the unconscious mind is the goal getter. Your unconscious mind is not out to get you – rather, it's out TO GET FOR YOU whatever you want in life. If you are not precisely clear about what you want, it will keep bringing you those thoughts you have in your conscious mind. This is so important to understand. Your unconscious mind only does what it thinks you want! It is in fact your Golden Key to unlock the door into your own desired world.

We have all grown up with rules on 'how things should be' and this controls our habitual behaviours. It is as if these rules are set in stone. Different families and different countries have different rules. We need to understand that it is only in the mind that these rules exist. Your life stems from your mind and when we truly understand the meaning of this, then we really are in control of our lives. You can send out the message that you want to be wealthy. This vibration will come back to you and give you what you want. There are particular ways the vibrations you send out into the universe are required, for this to become your reality. They have to be very precise and need to be studied.

It is not enough to 'wish' you were wealthy or achieved your goal, because that is the outcome you will attract – you will always be stuck at 'wishing'. The Universe is vastly intelligent, so think of it as similar to a computer. What goes out from you will come back to you – crucial fact.

"You create your own universe as you go along"
—Winston Churchill[161]

With that in mind let us now turn our attention on how to create wealth be it financial or achievement in other ways.

You now know that your outgoing vibrations can and will become a reality and that the Universe will present ways to you, when the time is right, to respond precisely to your thoughts.

There is a Secret Formula which can bring fortunes to those who truly are ready, but even more importantly, who understand. An odd thing about this Secret is that those who acquire it and use it are swept onto success. This Secret does have a price – those who are not intentionally searching for it cannot ever have it, but it serves those who are ready for it, bringing to them whatever is truly desired, be it money, fame, recognition, health or happiness. All the people who have used *The Secret* have achieved success in whichever area they have chosen. Education has no bearing whatsoever on understanding The Secret. It only requires those that are ready and able to grasp it and use it.

All people experience problems in their life in earning a living and trying to find hope, courage and contentment as well as peace of mind. Acquiring riches is a means to enjoy a greater freedom in how we live. Remember all achievement, all earned riches have their beginning in an idea. If you are ready for The Secret then you already have the empowering energy of thought and will go on to recognise other information that will come to you. You will come to know how you can have, be, or do anything you want, know what you are capable of and who you really are. You will come to know the true magnificence that awaits your life.

The truth is simply "Think and Grow Rich". This is the title of a book written by Napolean Hill who was a protégé of Andrew Carnegie[162], who gave him the task of looking at what was the common path taken by all successful people. He gathered the life experiences of more than 500 men who had accumulated a huge amount of riches or success in many fields, men who even began in poverty, with little education or influence.

He discovered there was definitely a route they followed. He has written about these and set them out in detail in his book.

I have set out some of the most necessary steps he shows that need to be followed. His book is worth a read to get the full picture. A great deal of this information comes from the ancient wisdom contained in 'The Secret'[163].

Steps to achieve Wealth & Success

To begin, keep asking, 'What do I want?' 'What do I really want to change in my life?' You need to be clear. Spend a great deal of time asking yourself this question until you are clear in your mind the precise nature of what you really want. This might even take some weeks. Once you are clear you can move on.

#1 Belief

You need to know in your whole being, that you are NOW, in this time of successful achievement, whatever that means to you. Feel the experience of being successful as you walk around in whatever you are engaged in. Do not be put off by any evidence to the contrary. Talk to yourself and feel the energy you are creating in believing this. Live in this aura of the success of your achievement. You are now already halfway there when you feel the elation and the energy of this state! Maintain this all the time. You will be amazed at how you 'see' things from this perspective. Your life will really feel buoyant. Your mind will also be open to possibilities.

#2 Desire

Now focus on what you DESIRE. Do not at this stage dwell on HOW you will obtain it. Remember thought is energy and energy is power. This power house is all we need to access what it is you desire, be it health, harmony, abundance or whatever else you want to achieve for your welfare and happiness. The start of achieving any goal is to Create a Burning Desire, an all-consuming Burning Desire which 'attaches' to the end result of where you want to be.

#3 Visualisation

Now turn your attention to Visualising how your life will be with these desired goals. This is the next most important step to integrate into your whole vibrating self. Visualise the events, circumstances and conditions which will be yours. Visualisation really sets the scene you desire. It will give it substance, colour and the lifestyle you will eventually have. Include the activities, where you will live and importantly what you are able to do in that setting. Let your mind enjoy your creativity. Do not hold back, enjoy and feel the exhilaration, no holds barred! The sky is the limit – truly.

#4 Focus

A Burning Desire is the beginning, Visualising is next and now you are ready to take this next important step – Focus. Keep your end result always at the forefront of your mind. Focus is the driving force in achieving your outcome. See yourself on the path towards your goal and tune in to the work you now need to do. You will be introduced to what you need to do. The way will be shown to you and lead to you knowing the steps needed to achieve them. It is a process. It is learning. It develops and your understanding of the path and the achievement of your end goal will be revealed. Your world 'within' will become your world 'without' and life will respond to your every wish in the manner best suited. This Universal Law of Attraction is an indisputable Law. We are but channels for the Universe to achieve the greatest good. We need to open ourselves up to be that channel without doubts or fears.

Let us take the example of all great athletes. They have to work hard to achieve their chosen goal. They work at this all the time in their training programs, focussing on the end result, and so it is with every achievement – clarifying what you need to know – to achieve your goal. All those who have achieved their goals, have had this driving force and steadfast resolve to stay with their focus and not rest until satisfied. This can be applied to all areas of life and means that all is attainable. It all starts within our mind.

#5 Clarity

Essentially it is necessary to set the exact situation or amount of money you will have as your goal, and importantly, to state why you want this and what you hope to achieve with it. There is no right or wrong. It is whatever you desire. This will be setting out your 'garden' in which the 'seeds' of your wealth will be sown. Your very own 'Garden of Paradise' so to speak. Make a drawing or a collage, if that is appealing to you and includes in it all you desire. Then set out clearly some real goals that will be achieved. You can change it as your mind becomes accustomed to setting goals and you become clearer in your thoughts.

Write them down. Place them where you will see them every day. Live with these thoughts and become so desirous of them that they become like an obsession. The energy and vibrations that you will be sending out into the Universe, will be very powerful.

#6 Planning

Now include a plan to achieve these goals. What lengths are you prepared to go to in order to achieve this? There is no such thing as something for nothing. What information will you need? What skills can you get that are appropriate to achieve your goal? Remember all successful people work obsessively towards their goals and do whatever is necessary to achieve them, learning about the subject in whatever way is necessary. Set out your chosen plan and when obstacles present just change tack. Sometimes we can achieve things by not going via the most direct route. I have a story that will illustrate this – on taking an indirect route and on never giving up and which has led me to a saying that I often use now: "If there isn't a front door entry to what you want to achieve, then try a back door"!

One of my sons had a beautiful singing voice and had had singing lessons. When it came to his 11 plus exam he failed (first set back). Now I knew this little chap was intelligent and that he also wanted to go to the local grammar school. It just so happened that we lived near a Cathedral School, which was a fee paying Direct Grant Grammar School which took in Choristers and gave them a free education, if they were chosen as Choirboys. I was not in any position to pay for his education so this seemed a likely route. He attended a singing audition for the choir, but failed (second set back). However there happened to be a Music Festival later that summer and a part of it was in singing. I entered him for this.

One person on the panel was the choirmaster from the Choir School who had previously turned him down as a chorister. My son's chosen song was "Shine out Great Sun". He sang it without fault and with such good feeling, all accentuated by the fact that a thunderstorm began to rage outside, much to the amusement of all in the hall! He walked away with the first prize of his year. I approached this same choir master afterwards and he was gracious enough to then accept him into the choir. My son then went onto Oxford and achieved a 'first' in History. An 11+ failure led to gaining a first at Oxford! All because we persisted and found 'the back door'.

However I need to add that the choristers had to work very long hours, stay for practice after school finished for the day and particularly attend the services on Sundays in the morning and evening. His scholarly achievement was obtained through a lot of hard work and discipline. This discipline was good training for the rest of his life – to achieve what he set his mind to. He had set his heart on a goal and achieved it.

#7 Faith

This element will add to the vibrations of your thought and so connect to the Infinite Intelligence. This strong vibration of never wavering will induce a response in your subconscious mind. When you have faith, you will achieve. The Universe is vastly intelligent and gives us what we want when the time is right. It just needs you to be in the right place in your mind and ready to receive, however long that may take. Opportunities will be presented to you and unless you are ready for them you will not recognise them and they will pass by. When you are ready and open you will recognise them with joy. So have an abundance of Faith in the achievement of your goal.

Financial Education

I am adding a word here about schools and how we are not educated about money in our formative years. This is a serious omission. Financial literacy is fundamental to the greater understanding and achievement of wealth. Money without Financial literacy is soon gone. Robert Kyosaki[164] is very clear on this point; "It is not how much money you make, it is how you manage it and how much you keep". Money needs sound management.

As our schools do not give any good grounding in how to obtain money nor indeed on how to manage it, our basic education about money is ignored. This means that children are not prepared for the real world where money is at the core and is the means to achieve any desired standard of living. Financial 'education' as such, is usually picked up by the child from its parents. If the parents have also not had any financial learning then whatever ways the parents manage, or not, their methods will be passed onto the children. Robert Kyosaki has even made the statement that he I believes "schools are actually teaching people how to be poor" and he goes on to say that "there are ways to obtain wealth and gain freedom, away from the mainstream daily 'job' we are encouraged to train for".

A great many see the attainment of money as the means to go out and buy goods. Similarly, stories abound about those who were on a low income, received millions in the Lottery, but lo and behold in a few short months they were once again in poverty. Money without financial literacy is soon gone. Our spending habits reflect who we are. Robert Kyosaki states that those who are poor, are people who have not learnt any other way, other than to spend it, and consequently remain poor.

Information about this important matter of money is seen as belonging to those who have undergone further education in the subject and so trust is given to Bank Managers, Financial Advisors, Stock Brokers etc. who of course all create their wealth from other people's money. Anyone can achieve prosperity and financial acumen if they search for it. The internet has developed in many ways, so information on any subject is now readily available. However, beware of the many sharks who want to take your hard-earned cash.

Robert Kiyosaki has written a good book on Financial Education, called *"Rich Dad Poor Dad"*. This was based on his life's experiences of seeing how one Dad, who was always financially Poor (his real Dad) and another Rich (His best friend's Dad with whom he spent time, listened to and who he 'adopted'). He was able to compare the two very different ways in which each spoke about, used and understood money. He learnt what the Rich teach their children, and came to fully understand why his Poor Dad was always in debt, although he had had a good education and held down a professional job. Eventually with the education from his Rich Dad he came to a real understanding about what money really is and how to manage it. He learned that it is a commodity to be used, and more importantly he learned how to use it, so that it increased. He was able to become immensely rich with this knowledge. He passes on all this information in his book. He learned that the rich acquire assets while the middle class acquire liabilities. An asset is something that puts money in your pocket. A liability is something that takes money out. A good standard for the meaning of Wealth, is that it means having enough to cover all expenses each month. Being Rich means you have a great deal and more than enough, in financial terms, to meet those requirements. The single most valuable asset we have is our mind, which is really our only tool to create tremendous wealth because wealth as we know, does not fall from the trees. Finding the 'right' path is your mind mission.

Robert Kyosaki's financial path is not one that will suit all but the principles show how it is possible for anyone, who has the desire, to become very wealthy by following the steps to achieve this. These principles are also contained in *"The Secret"* and are rock hard. Times have changed in terms of technical availability, but it is still true that financial education is very important because money needs to be managed, whatever age we live in. It must be noted that all the great and wealthy who have known and understood *"The Secret"*, have all succeeded. People such as; Plato, Shakespeare, Newton, Victor Hugo, Beethoven, Lincoln, Emerson, Edison, Einstein, Bill Gates, Richard Branson, to name but a few.

> *"The Secret is the answer to all that has been, all there is, and all that will ever be"*
>
> —Ralph Waldo Emerson[165]

I recently watched a TV program where a member of the Inuit was searching for ancient Rhino horns buried by the side of a river bed. He happened to say "If a man sets himself on a path and keeps to it, then he will succeed" I wonder if he had read *"The Secret"*? I doubt it, but he knew this fundamental truth for sure and he worked steadfastly towards his goal, overcoming many physical obstacles on the way. The program went on to show how he eventually succeeded in finding enough Rhino Horns to create a sufficient income. I was impressed with this man's wisdom and focus.

As a person it is perfectly possible that you now have the power to never again feel helpless, never on the defensive and never needing to depend on anyone or anything. You can enter a new world, control your own future, gain real power over your life and profit greatly from it. There are practical tools to help you on the right track. No need to stay where you are, if it does not suit you, no need to be in a draining and stressful life. Through understanding and using these tools for yourself you will experience a mounting sense of power and excitement when applying each of these principles. These principles are based on a fully integrated honesty. They are rooted in effort, objective reality and value production – the keys to manifestation. These tools efficiently deliver prosperity and happiness through planning, effort, discipline and thought control. A happy cheerful world is created by individuals who prosper by producing value for others as it is the moral code – that which is consciously done to help fill human biological needs. The maxim that life is good, oneself and others are good encourages this and is the means by which we develop a worthy and fruitful living.

This Law of Abundance is another fundamental and Natural Law of the Universe – there is ample money for everyone who knows how to acquire it and keep it. This Law, as well as any other Universal Law is no respecter of persons but it is in constant operation, relentlessly bringing to each individual exactly what he has created. "Whatever a man soweth – so shall he reap". Those who recognise and understand this Law of Abundance and who place themselves in harmony with it, need to adhere to certain mental and moral codes of practice; Courage, loyalty, tact, goodness, individuality and constructiveness. These are the modes of thought and are the conditions that are required in making contact with the Universal Intelligence. Opportunities will come when in this frame of mind, as soon as we are ready for them. Our current time frame may not be the one best suited. The Universe will deliver when the time is right.

Understand we all have the means of tapping into the Great Cosmic Intelligence and attracting from it that which links with the ambitions and aspirations of each of us. Let us examine this further.

We have seen that human thought is the spiritual power of the universe, which actually operates through us all and that all we desire, must first be created in thought, to become a reality. Think about it. Everything starts with a thought. A painting a piece of furniture a machine – all these began with a thought and then through a concentration of effort and dedication – became reality. This process of creation is carried on through definite and scientific laws. We create everything with our consciousness. There is nothing that would appear in your physical reality unless it had already existed in your thoughts or feelings. You might think that it is some external action that produced the result, and so you go about trying to change it. But your external action would not have taken place if it wasn't initially created by your mentality and emotions. If your consciousness was different, you would receive a different set of results even if you had taken the same actions. It is indisputable then, that every thought tends to become a material thing. Our desires are seeds of thought that then sprout and grow and blossom and then bear fruit. We are sowing these seeds every day. Today is a result of past thinking and later we will be the result of what we are now thinking. This is the Fundamental Law of Attraction. This law of mental attraction is as strong as the law between the atoms, which is so strong that when split apart, an enormous explosion occurs. Since mental currents are as real and as strong, know that our thoughts are, as in the grand nature of our world, very powerful. When we really understand that the mind is the great creative power, then by definition, all is possible. We can only receive what we give and it will only be received by those who can receive. Many do not fully understand this principle, do not perceive the opportunities that come their way and so stay stuck where they are in their mind structure. At this point please take a moment to pause and think back to times that changed your circumstances. I would like to share some experiences I have had, that really underline what I am about to reveal. I call them: "The Angels in my Life".

    I have had some very difficult times from an early age, but looking back I remember that there was always someone, not necessarily anyone I previously knew, who stepped into my life, maybe for just a brief moment, maybe with a one sentence remark, which showed me another way and significantly changed my life. There have been others, even comparative strangers who have given me their time and emotionally supported me. They have 'appeared' when I needed them most. A new path has always resulted because of these very special 'angels'. I can look back and count at least six such angels in my life who have been very influential. I also learnt a very valuable lesson from one of them. I asked her how I could ever repay her for what she had done for me (which by the way had been a lot over several weeks). Her remark has always stayed with me. "When you are in a position to help someone, then do so, that will be my reward and it is a way of passing love around the world". At the time I was not in any position to help anyone only just being able to hold my head above 'water' to avoid sinking into the downward spiral of no job and poverty, and not knowing if I would ever rise above this. She never gave me money, but practical help and support. That statement has stayed with me over these many years since then, so now when I am able to give some service, I will say the same to anyone who asks me how they can repay me. I really like that notion, it has a different energy to it.

I am sure if you were to look back you will also be able to recognise the 'angels in your life' A golden rule to follow to create light, love, and the good things in the world for yourself, is to give for the benefit to others and never to cause any harm. The golden key to giving is that the more that you give, the more you will receive. But give with love, without any thought of receiving, as otherwise it is trading.

> *"We make a living by what we get, but we make a life by what we give"*
>
> —Winston Churchill

If you first have the right consciousness for your desired results, it will cause you to take the right external actions which will then lead to your desired results. Be aware and in charge of your consciousness at all times rather than your actions. When you focus on your consciousness in everything you do, you will find that the doing becomes increasingly effortless and faster. Always look at what is within your own consciousness, because that is what creates everything else.

Be not discouraged – if you are starting out on a path to develop a business or a project – by those who do not 'see' what you are offering.

Find those who can receive!! They are like precious Jewels among the many unresponsive stones.

Nothing will reach us except when we are ready to receive and is necessary for our growth. All conditions and experiences that come to us do so for our own benefit. Difficulties and 'failures' are necessary for us to learn. We are on a journey of learning and we are being given those opportunities to develop from them. Once the lesson has been learnt we are then able to take up the next challenge. We are on a life's education course and it is up to each of us to learn and develop and then move on. If we are able to take up these challenges and work at overcoming them we will achieve. Look upon all setbacks and so called 'failures' as gifts. We are being educated! Understand this and your life's training will be joyous and lead to your own qualification and the achievement of your desires.

We now know that mental power is creative power, as it gives you the ability to create for yourself. This does not mean taking away from someone else. Nature does not work that way. Being in tune with the Universal Law of Abundance enables one to access this. Every thought we have, passes onto our subjective feeling brain which lies in the solar plexus or 'tummy' area. You know when you have problems about something or someone because you will 'feel' unease inside you. We all experience this 'gut feeling' at times, when things just don't 'feel right'. It is important to notice such feelings, because when there is discord, we need to acknowledge to ourselves quietly and honestly, how we feel and so be true to ourselves and others. Some people's actions or behaviour will generate either a good or bad feeling. This is your barometer, as it were, to help you make decisions on how to respond. We need to act with a clear conscience and with good vibrational energy, to send out to the universe into the cosmic intelligence. Listen to your most silent voice, and let your ego (body and mind) work, based only upon this very silent but truthful voice.

Stay away from people or situations that generate these unpleasant gut feelings. They do you no good. When you are in touch with your life force in your solar plexus, this will radiate life, energy and vitality to every part of your body and to all who you are in contact with. The body is then filled with happiness and health, as it basks in the life force of this energy. This is the condition where all is possible and there is no limit to what can be achieved since it is in contact with all life and intelligence. This gives power to the conscious mind. The quality of thought we entertain determines the nature of the outcome. Every thought brings into action certain physical changes in the brain, nerves and muscles, which then produce an actual physical change in the construction of the body tissue.

One of the biggest causes of health disorders is never having enough money as it creates stress, which we have seen how this is very damaging to our physical health. It is only necessary to have a certain number of thoughts on a given subject in order to bring about a complete change in the physical organisation of the body good or bad. We achieve all with our mind, both in health and achievement. It is an indisputable fact of the Law of the Universe and the way we use our vibrational power. It is The Law of Being which produces all conditions in the lives of men and women. We have already learnt that the mind is creative and operates through the Law of Attraction; 'what we send out we get back'. Everyone has the right to choose this gift to create. So the energy of theses good and creative thoughts we send out, will return in that which is attracted to us. This is the fundamental Law of Attraction. "You get what you give." The person who is radiating courage, belief, confidence and power will overcome all barriers and any doubts expressed by others, will have no impact. This understanding is the cornerstone from which our future is built and it is the foundation of all that is to come. So mentally concentrate on the object of your desire and the vibrations will strengthen and become a force without bounds. Every person, in whatever situation, who understands these laws, will succeed, as have others, in the past. Our thoughts are part of the Universal Mind, the Universal Intelligence and we need to access this all the time in our thoughts for the wealth and happiness we so deserve.

As each one of us is part of the universe, any attempt to profit by the ignorance or necessity of another will inevitably operate to one's disadvantage. The welfare of each part depends upon the recognition of the interest of the whole and those who recognise this principle have a great advantage in the affairs of life and do not waste their money or time upon objects which can be of no possible benefit to themselves or others. If you decide to do something, then do it. Start with small chunks that you can achieve and as you proceed, maintain the focus of what you desire. Through this you will receive creative thoughts to help you in your end result and ways will open up as you walk towards your earnest and focussed desire.

You now understand how these Universal Laws are there for you as well as others. Knowing how to use them is the lesson. The Law of Being is manifest by creating your own world. The mind is the one great cause which produces all conditions in the lives of men and women. The mind is creative and operates through the Law of Attraction. You are on your own chosen journey of life. Enjoy the challenges and especially the rewards. Remember the Universe is there for YOU.

> *"You are a child of the universe, no less than the trees and the stars; you have a right to be here. And whether or not it is clear to you, no doubt the universe is unfolding as it should."*
> —Max Ehrmann, Desiderata: A Poem for a Way of Life

Learning is the beginning of wealth.

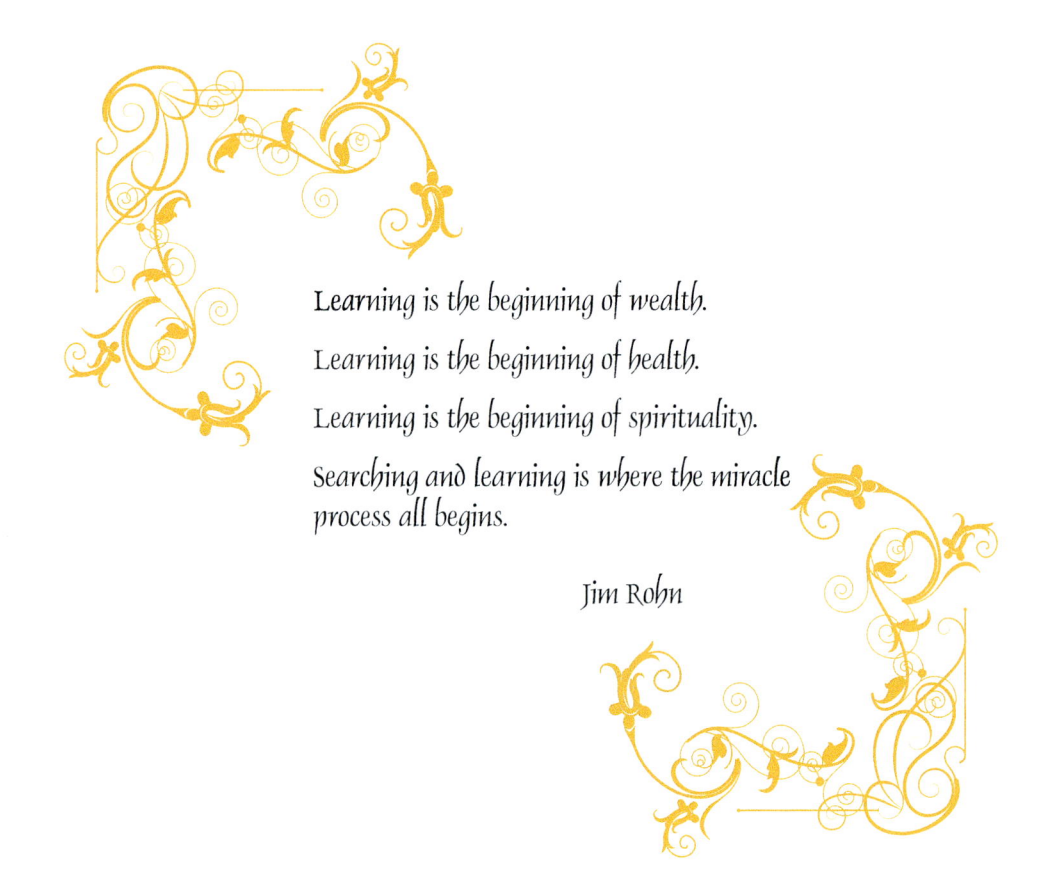

Learning is the beginning of health.

Learning is the beginning of spirituality.

Searching and learning is where the miracle process all begins.

> Jim Rohn

Summary

Dear reader,

In the introduction I posed a question as to whether another way, could be found to manage the increased burden on the burgeoning costs to our Health Service.

Our Health Service is reactive to the many demands being made on it. It deals with ill health in the hope that the treatment given will put people back on their feet in order that they may continue living in a productive and happy manner.

I have set out in the previous pages many ways that ill health and disease can, to a large extent, be prevented and how, natural and well researched ways can help to facilitate such prevention.

If the main causes of disease are due to lifestyle and the ignorance surrounding the many ways our immune system is being compromised, then this, I suggest is where the focus needs to be. Prevention is, after all, always better than cure.

Sustaining our health with this knowledge and understanding of how and what to avoid, in our present toxic environment, is also vitally important and the real bedrock for health maintenance.

In addition, we now know that there are ways to balance our natural flow of energy, this being so very necessary to our wellbeing, and of vital importance in the maintenance of sound health.

All these considerations need to be taken into account in offering ways to affect and achieve a healthful and positive outcome in health matters.

Our free health care system is something the public have come to respect and also expect. People have paid for it with their National Insurance contributions throughout their working lives and are then reluctant to bear any further costs to obtain health care. Many do not have either the financial means, have knowledge of, or have access to 'other ways' that are available. Health care at present is seen to be largely the responsibility of the Health Service and not necessarily of the individual. Overall, these reasons are the real deterrents for people in embracing the many health enhancing methods available.

It seems that there is a strong case for an additional and government-funded health preventative arm of the Health Service, which would include Health Education and Maintenance. This would be a proactive addition to our current Health Service, focussing, as the title suggests, on all matters relating to the education, maintenance and enhancement of health. This over the years would be cost effective by reducing the burden on the current NHS and more importantly, over time, could lead to a healthier nation. Education leads to knowledge and then to change. Parts 2, 3, 4 and 5 show the many ways this could be addressed.

Part 6 specifically includes how each person can initiate and take a proactive position for their own health. Part 7 identifies, how with the availability of health supporting equipment, this will further assist in the enhancement and maintenance of sound health. Additional health promoting methods, as identified in Part 8, would further complement this whole process.

Health Practices, identified in Part 9, would be managed by qualified practitioners, many of whom might well include medical doctors who wish to focus on this particular health education and maintenance side of our National Health Service. Referrals could be made between these two arms of the Health Service.

Stress from whatever cause affects all the cells in our body and leads to ill health. Poverty and living in a negative or abusive environment can be a real source of stress. Part 10 sets out a well-trodden path, followed by many people, who have also overcome adversity and then risen to achieve success in their chosen paths. Embracing this, for Your Life, is now Your Choice.

I thank you for taking the time to read these pages.

Yours,

Gretchen Pyves.

Notes and References

NOTES FOR PREFACE
1. Napolean Hill. Author of "Think and Grow Rich" Revised by Arthur R Pell. ISBN:0091900212.

NOTES FOR PART 1
2. Beveridge Report – Search – Beveridge Report 1942
http://www.bbc.co.uk/history/ww2peopleswar/timeline/factfiles/nonflash/a1143578.shtml
3. The Kings Fund: Health Promotion and Ill-health prevention – 2010
https://www.kingsfund.org.uk/sites/default/files/field/field_document/health-promotion-ill-health-prevention-gp-inquiry-research-paper-mar11.pdf
4. What Doctors Don't Tell You (WDDTY) Dec 2017

NOTES FOR PART 2
5. Hans Selye's natural philosophy of life. The social and scientific origins of 'The pursuit of Happiness'
https://www.ncbi.nlm.nih.gov/pmc/articles/PMC3724273/

Further reading
The Immune System Cure: Optimize Your Immune System in 30 Days – the Natural Way, authors Lorna Vanderhaeghe and Patrick J.D. Bouic, Ph.D.,
The Immune System Cure: Optimize Your Immune System in 30 Days – the Natural Way, authors Lorna Vanderhaeghe and Patrick J.D. Bouic, Ph.D.,
https://www.nutrex-hawaii.com/blogs/learn/the-immune-system-explained
Lauren M. Sompayrac : "How the immune system works". (Amazon: 'Lauren Sompayrac immune')
The Immune System Explained: https://www.youtube.com/watch?v=zQGOcOUBi6s
Tim Newman 2018 "How the immune system works" Medical News Today
https://www.ncbi.nlm.nih.gov/pmc/articles/PMC3724273/
CAMS. Complementary and alternative medicine. (CAMS) https://www.nhs.uk/conditions/complementary-and-alternative-medicine/#cams-and-the-nhs
Alliance for Natural Health 09 Aug 2011
http://www.anh-usa.org/readers-corner-can-doctor-get-into-trouble-offering-natural-treatments/
Health Services Research journal. 15 Sep 2011
https://www.sott.net/article/235021-Doctors-Use-Natural-Remedies-But-Don-t-Prescribe-Them-

Stress

Further Reading

"Stress Management Approaches for Preventing and Reducing Stress" Harvard health Publications, Harvard Medical School
https://www.health.harvard.edu/mind-and-mood/stress-management-enhance-your-well-being-by-reducing-stress-and-building-resilience

Infection

6. Alexander Tomasz PhD serves as Member of Scientific Advisory Board at Exponential Biotherapies, Inc. serves as Chair of Bacteriology at The Rockefeller University and is a prominent infectious disease specialist.

Further Reading

Restore Gut health: http://www.integratedhealth.com/supplements/probioyics-enzymes-foods/restore-for-gut-health.html
Antibiotic Resistance: http://www.who.int/mediacentre/commentaries/antibiotic-resistance/en/
www.nhs.uk/nhsengland/arc/pages/aboutarc.aspx
https://energymedicineforlife.wordpress.com/2015/03/15/energy-medicine-albert-einstein-and-you/

Pollutants

7. Professor Dame Sally Davies England's Chief Medical Officer Report. March 2017/2018
https://www.gov.uk/government/publications/chief-medical-officer-annual-report-2017-health-impacts-of-all-pollution-what-do-we-know

Chemicals

8. Dr William L Marcus: http://www.infraredsauna.co.uk/detoxification/

Antibiotics

9. Dr Keith Scott-Mumby. "Fire in the Belly". The surprise cause of most diseases. (Published by Mother Whale inc) http://fireinthebellybook.com/1sc/
10. The British Medical Journal. May 12. 1917 Moris Malcolm: "The therapeutic effects of Colloidal Preparations".
10. The British Medical Journal 1932 Colloidal Silver. Preparation of Silver in Pharmacy.
https://www.quantumbalancing.com/news/cs_historical.htm
11. WilliamTiller Ph.D. Psychoenergetic Science Applied to The Mind-Body Concept. [September 2010] https://www.youtube.com/watch?v=fO4vcxD2_Wg
12. George Crile. MD: Founder of the Cleveland Clinic 1864 1943. Formally recognized as the first surgeon to have succeeded in a direct blood transfusion.
https://energymedicineforlife.wordpress.com/2015/03/15/energy-medicine-albert-einstein-and-you/
13. Albert Einstein. A German-born theoretical physicist who developed the theory of relativity, one of the two pillars of modern physics.
https://energymedicineforlife.wordpress.com/2015/03/15/energy-medicine-albert-einstein-and-you/
14. Bolazs Bodai Director of the Breast Cancer Survivorship Institute in Sacramento California. Reported in WDDTY Dec 2017

Further Reading

Restore Gut Health: http://www.integratedhealth.com/supplements/probiotics-enzymes-foods/restore-for-gut-health.html

Antibiotic Resistance: http://www.who.int/mediacentre/commentaries/antibiotic-resistance/en/
www.nhs.uk/nhsengland/arc/pages/aboutarc.aspx

Further Reading on Colloidal Silver
Duncan Martha. Several Reports on Colloidal Silver. The Best Kept Secret.: http://www.dazer.com/silver-1.html
http://www.silver-water.net/more-reading-on-coillidal-silver.html
http://www.alternative-health-group.org/colloidal-silver.php

Over the counter medicines
15. What Doctors Don't Tell You (WDDTY May 2018) The effects of painkillers.
16. What Doctors Don't Tell You (WDDTY May 2015) Chemical Process

Skin care/Cosmetics
17. Journal of the American College of Toxicology, Volume 2, Number 7 1983. "Dangers of Sodium Lauryl Sulfate" https://www.livestrong.com
http://www.healthy-communications.com/journal_of_the_american_college_.html
18. Environmental Working Group's Skin Deep Cosmetic Safety Database, https://www.livestrong.com/article/174367-dangers-of-sodium-lauryl-sulfate/

Further Reading
Livestrong.com, August 16, 2013, Shannon Marks, "Skin Lotion Ingredients to Avoid," https://www.homecuresthatwork.com/22121/8-dangerous-chemicals-in-your-body-care-products/.
Environmental Health Insights: Published online 2015 Nov 17. https://www.ncbi.nlm.nih.gov/pmc/articles/PMC4651417/
Damaging effects of Cosmetics: https://listovative.com/top-15-harmful-side-effects-of-using-cosmetics/
Sodium Lauryl Sulphate.Learn the Facts: https://slsfree.net/
SLS & Cancer: https://www.livestrong.com/article/458074-does-sodium-laureth-sulfate-cause-cancer/

Aluminium
19. Dr Daniel Krewski et al. Human Health Risk Assessment for Aluminium. https://uknowledge.uky.edu/cgi/viewcontent.cgi?referer=https://www.google.co.uk/&httpsredir=1&article=1051&context=ps_facpub
20. Dr Edward Group: https://www.globalhealingcenter.com/natural-health/why-you-should-use-aluminum-free-deodorant/

Fluoride
21. Dr. Edward Group DC, NP, DACBN, DCBCN, Published on March 26, 2009, Fluoride Last Updated on November 16, 2015 https://www.globalhealingcenter.com/natural-health/how-safe-is-fluoride/
22. Dr Dean Burke. (March 21, 1904–October 6, 1988) http://www.ign.com/boards/threads/dr-dean-burk-fluoride-causes-cancer.452774459/
22. Dr Dean Burke- Video: https://www.youtube.com/watch?v=r7CxjCHf4R8
23. Dr Mercola : https://articles.mercola.com/sites/articles/archive/2013/04/30/water-fluoridation-facts.aspx
24. The Lancet on Fluoride. VOLUME 13, ISSUE 7, P647-648, JULY 01, 2014

Care of the Teeth
25. Periodontal Disease: What Doctors Don't Tell you.- WDDTY February 2016

Further reading
Michael Connett "10 Fluoride Facts You Should Know" 30 April 2013
https://todaynews2.com/tag/is-fluoride-bad-for-you-fluoride-facts
Periodontal Disease: What Doctors Don't Tell you. February 2016

Household Cleaners
26. Philip Dickey Washington Toxics Coalition
https://www.globalhealingcenter.com/about/dr-group
27. National Institute of Occupational Safety and Health. (NIOSH)
https://www.cdc.gov/niosh/topics/indoorenv/chemicalsodors.html

Electro-magnetic Fields
28. Robert O Becker DR. EMF pioneer and Nobel prize nominee: "The Body Electric" 1 Jan 1985
Dr Robert Becker. https://flutuante.wordpress.com/2013/09/01/the-invisible-carcinogenic-pollution/
29. Dr Pawluk: https://www.drpawluk.com/education/magnetic-science/biomagnetic-fields/
Geopathic Stress: http://www.helios3.com/geopathic-stress.html
30. Jeff Jeffries: https://www.intelligentenergies.com/geopathic-stress/

Cell Phones
31. David Carpenter, MD, Professor, Environmental Health Sciences, and Director of the Institute for Health and the Environment, School of Public Health, University of Albany. "Health Effects of Electromagnetic Fields". Dec 2014
32. Samuel Milham MD. MPH "Dirty Electricity: Electrification and the Diseases of Civilization" Dec 2012
Samuel Milham MD. MCH – Video: https://www.youtube.com/watch?v=zI6VhS_QCJ0
33. Andrew Weil MD and EMF Pollution. Author of "8 Weeks to Optimum health & Spontaneous healing" ISBN 9780345498021
Andrew Weil: https://emfblues.com/electromagnetic-protection/

Further reading – cell phones
Lloyd Morgan, BS Electronic Engineering, Senior Research Fellow with the Environmental Health Trust https://www.electricsense.com/8486/interview-emf-expert-brain-tumor-survivor-lloyd-morgan/
Environmental Health Trust web site: https://ehtrust.org/
10 Tips to reduce cell phone radiation: https://ehtrust.org/take-action/educate-yourself/10-things-you-can-do-to-reduce-the-cancer-risk-from-cell-phones/

Microwave ovens
34. Hans Hertel cited in: https://www.mercola.com/article/microwave/hazards2.htm
35. "Dangers of Microwave Ovens": https://www.safespaceprotection.com/news-and-info/microwave-oven-dangers/
36. The Lancet 1989. Lubec et al : https://advancednaturopathic.com/two-problems-with-microwaving-food/
37. David Carpenter: https://goop.com/wellness/food-planet/dr-david-carpenter-on-why-we-need-more-research-on-cell-phone-safety/
38. Lloyd Morgan, BS Electronic Engineering, Senior Research Fellow with the Environmental Health Trust https://www.electricsense.com/8486/interview-emf-expert-brain-tumor-survivor-lloyd-morgan/

Further reading
The Guardian: https://guardian.ng/features/health/scientists-call-for-protection-from-ill-health-effects-of-cell-phones-wi-fi/
British Society of Ecological Medicine – (Video worth watching): https://vimeo.com/100623585
Clinton Ober, StephenT, Sinatra. MD, Martin Zucker. "Earthing" 2010. ISBN 978-1-59120-283-7
EM Radiation: http://www.helios3.com/electromagnetic-radiation-electrosensitivity.html
Martin Blank: "The Dangers of Electromagnetic Radiation" (EMF) ISBN: 978160985098
Natural Science-Microwave Ovens: https://www.naturalscience.org/topics/microwaves-mobile-communications/microwave-ovens/
Dangers of Microwave Ovens: https://www.safespaceprotection.com/news-and-info/microwave-oven-dangers/
NCBI-Recent advances of Microwave Radiation on Brains: https://www.ncbi.nlm.nih.gov/pmc/articles/PMC5607572/

NOTES FOR PART 3

39. The Blue Zones: https://en.wikipedia.org/wiki/Blue_Zone
40. The Hunza Tribes: http://thepdi.com/hunza_health_secrets.htm
41. Dr. Jean-Pierre Willem. "The Keys to extraordinary Longevity" ISBN 10: 1903904315 Date: 2003

Fast Foods
42. MSG in Foods: What Doctors Don't Tell You (WDDTY) 19 Nov 2012
43. Danilo Alfaro : https://www.thespruce.com/monosodium-glutamate-or-msg-996134
44. Peggy Trowbridge Filippone. https://www.thespruce.com/what-is-monosodium-glutamate-1809323

Trans Fats
45. James Marin. R. D https://www.beachbodyondemand.com/blog/what-are-trans-fats
46. Fred Kummerow, Dr of Biochemistry "Cholesterol Is Not the Culprit: A Guide to Preventing Heart Disease." ISBN: 9780983383567. Available from Amazon's Book Store.
47. Ancel Keys Ed. "A multivariate analysis of death and coronary heart disease". Seven Countries Study ISBN: 0-674-80237-3, 1980
48. Nina Teicholz July 2015 "The Big Fat Surprise – Why Butter, Meat and Cheese belong in a Healthy Diet" ISBN 9781925228106

Saturated Fats
49. Homocysteine: https://medical-dictionary.thefreedictionary.com/homocysteine
49. Dr Mercola – 7 Reasons to Eat more Saturated Fat: https://articles.mercola.com/sites/articles/archive/2009/09/22/7-reasons-to-eat-more-saturated-fat.aspx
49. Dr Mercola- Saturated fats are good for you: https://articles.mercola.com/sites/articles/archive/2011/09/01/enjoy-saturated-fats-theyre-good-for-you.aspx

Further reading
Dr Mercola: Reasons to eat more Saturated Fats https://articles.mercola.com/sites/articles/archive/2009/09/22/7-reasons-to-eat-more-saturated-fat.aspx

Soy Milk
50. Soy Side effects: http://www.stylecraze.com/articles/serious-side-effects-soy-proteins/#gref

Sweeteners
51.   Dangers of Aspartame: http://www.healthychoices.co.uk/aspartame.html
52.   Dr Susan Shiffman: https://www.prevention.com/food-nutrition/healthy-eating/a20464317/health-risks-of-sucralose/
52.   Dr. Susan Shiffman et al: Journal of Toxicology and Environmental Health. Part B, Critical Reviews https://www.ncbi.nlm.nih.gov/pmc/articles/PMC3856475/
53.   American Heart Association: https://www.heart.org/en/healthy-living/healthy-eating/eat-smart/sugar/added-sugars

Fruit Drinks
54.   Journal of Respirology. 2012 Feb;17 https://www.ncbi.nlm.nih.gov/pubmed/22142454
55.   Fruit Juice: https://www.healthline.com/nutrition/fruit-juice-is-just-as-bad-as-soda
55.   Fruit Drinks: https://www.quora.com/Is-Coca-Cola-dangerous-to-drink
55.   Video on Coca Cola: https://www.youtube.com/watch?v=gVyZiYbsvLY

Further reading
Energy and Sports Drinks: Health drinks British Columbia: https://www.healthlinkbc.ca/health-topics/abo4575
Caffeine users and side effects: https://www.webmd.com/vitamins/ai/ingredientmono-979/caffeine
Effects of Coke: https://healthprep.com/fitness-nutrition/6-things-that-happen-when-you-begin-drinking-coke-on-a-daily-basis/
Detoxing with Dr Group: http://drdetox.tv/

NOTES FOR PART 4

Smoking
56.   Lung Association newfoundland & Labrador:
https://www.charityintelligence.ca/charity-details/342-newfoundland-and-labrador-lung-association
57.   Krosnick J, Malhotra N, Mo CH. Bruera EF, Chang L, Pasek J7 Thomas RK. "Smoking: Risk, perception, and policy". Thousand Oaks, CA: Sage:
https://www.ncbi.nlm.nih.gov/pubmed/28806420

Further Reading
Smoking: Risk, Perception, and Policy:
https://books.google.co.uk/books/about/Smoking.html?id=GwZzAwAAQBAJ&redir_esc=y

Vaping
58.   Volume 1. Research "acute effects of using an electronic nicotine-delivery device (e-cigarette) on myocardial function: comparison with the effects of regular cigarettes by K. Farsalinos, D. Tsiapras, S. Kyrzopoulos, M. Savvopoulou, E. Avramidou, D. Vasilopoulou, V. Voudris, Onassis".
http://www.ecigclick.co.uk/e-cig-research/ecigarette-use-has-no-effect-on-oxygen-getting-to-the-heart/
59.   Volume 2. e-cigarettes as a source of toxic and potentially carcinogenic metals
https://www.ncbi.nlm.nih.gov/pmc/articles/PMC5135636/

Further reading
Journal: J.F. Pankow et al. Benzene formation in electronic cigarettes. PLOS ONE. March 8, 2017. doi: 10.1371/journal.pone.0173055.
Journal: W. Lei et al. Myofibroblast differentiation and its functional properties are inhibited

by nicotine and e-cigarette via mitochondrial OXPHOS complex III. Scientific Reports. Vol. 7, March 3, 2017. doi: 10.1038/srep43213.
Journal: C.A. Hess et al. E-cigarettes as a source of toxic and potentially carcinogenic metals. Environmental Research. Vol. 152, January 28, 2017, p. 221. doi: 10.1016/j.envres.2016.09.026.

Alcohol
60.   BBC Report on Alcohol: https://www.bbc.co.uk/news/health-35151246

Further Reading
Effects of Alcohol Abuse:
https://recovergateway.org/substance-abuse-resources/alcohol-addiction-effects/
Rehabs.com: https://luxury.rehabs.com/alcohol-addiction/alcohol/
NHS Choices. The Risks: https://www.nhs.uk/Livewell/alcohol/Pages/Effectsofalcohol.aspx

Illegal Drugs
61.   Natural ways to beat Addictions: https://www.organicfacts.net/drug-addiction.html

Further Reading
The Risks of Drugs https://luxury.rehabs.com/drug-addiction/dangers-of-drug-addiction/
National Institute on Drug abuse: https://www.drugabuse.gov/

Compulsive Buying Disorder
Compulsive Buying Disorder: When Shopping Addiction Becomes a Problem:
https://theoakstreatment.com/blog/shopping-addiction/
Project Know: https://www.projectknow.com/research/shopping-addiction/

Mobile phones
62.   Journal of Natural Science and Medicine https://www.ncbi.nlm.nih.gov/pmc/articles/PMC4934115/

Further Reading
Wikipedia on Mobile phones: https://en.wikipedia.org/wiki/Mobile_phone_overuse

Gambling
63.   The Guardian. August 2017. https://www.theguardian.com/society/2017/aug/24/problem-gamblers-uk-gambling-commission-report
64.   Gambling Addiction & Treatment : http://gamblingaddiction.org.uk/treatment.html

Notes for Part 5

65.   Dr John Bergman: https://www.youtube.com/watch?v=p3V3TITSDxc

Water
66.   Masaru Emoto: Dr of Alternative Medicine: "The Hidden messages in Water" Atria Books. ISBN – 13: 978-0-7432-8980-1
67.   Dr. Allen E Banik "The Choice is Clear" ISBN 0-911311-31-9
68.   Dr Anne Marie Mahon at the Galway-Mayo Institute of Technology, (Microplasics in water)
http://www.thatsfarming.com/news/plastic-water-research
69.   Paul Melia. June 8 2017: https://freshwatermicroplastics.com/featured-articles/the-independent/
70.   Distilled Water: www.h2olabs.co.uk/BestDistillers/PurestWater
71.   Dr. Zach Bush – 'How to Hydrate at Cellular level. Full explanation on Cellular Hydration'

https://articles.mercola.com/sites/articles/archive/2018/05/06/how-to-hydrate-at-the-cellular-level.aspx?utm_source=dnl&utm_medium=email&utm_content=art1&utm_campaign=2

Further Reading
https://www.theguardian.com/environment/2017/sep/06/plastic-fibres-found-tap-water-around-world-study-reveals
Also: https://www.independent.ie/news/environment/humans-at-risk-of-ingesting-microplastics-through-drinking-water-or-by-eating-certain-types-of-fish-research-35802684.html

Himalayan Rock Salt
72.   Dr Helen Smith: http://delibiromaniac.info/

Organic Food

Further Reading
Science Daily, February 21, 2018 (Oganic foods)
The Guardian February 10, 2015 British Journal of Nutrition 2014 Jun 26:1-18 (Organic Food)
Antibiotic Use for Farm Animals – microbewiki (A threat to Human health)
Encyclopedia of Foods and Their Healing Power (3 Volume Set): Hardcover – June 2004
www.hhesbiblestory.com/product/encyclopedia-of-foods-and-their-healing-power/
Medicinal Benefits of Whole Foods –
http://www.sheknows.com/health-and-wellness/articles/1098723/foods-that-have-medicinal-properties
NaturalWays: www.naturalways.com/medValFd.htm
The benefits of organic foods. https://www.helpguide.org/articles/healthy-eating/organic-foods.htm
The Daily Telgraph. Lifestyle Food & Drink.
https://www.telegraph.co.uk/food-and-drink/grow-a-healthier-family/benefits-of-eating-organic/
Brendan Salmon B.A. (Hons): "Natures Secrets- in Health & Vitality": ISBN 1 870703 17 0
Dr Andrew Dracea with Jackie Seguin: "Eat and Heal". Bodywell Holdings. SA, Nyon
Felicity Lawrence "Not on the Label" Penguin Books 2004

Food Supplements
73.   Robert Thompson MD & Kathleen Barnes "The Calcium Lie" ISBN: 978-0-98838-665-5
https://www.angiesoption.com/2015/02/the-vitamin-lie-an-indepth-look-at-vitamin-c/
74.   D Action Project: www.grassrootshealth.net also : www.vitamindsociety.org
75.   British Association of Dermatologists: http://www.bad.org.uk/for-the-public/skin-cancer/vitamin-d

Further Reading
Journal of Toxicology and Environmental Health, Part B: Critical Reviews. 17 Dec 2013
https://www.angiesoption.com/2015/02/the-vitamin-lie-an-indepth-look-at-vitamin-c/

Exercise
76.   CMAJ. JAMC March 2006: Health benefits of physical activity – the evidence:
https://www.ncbi.nlm.nih.gov/pmc/articles/PMC1402378/#__sec17tit
77.   Donna E.Shalala: Report on Physical Activity and Health:
https://www.cdc.gov/nccdphp/sgr/index.htm

Notes for Part 6

78. Fritz-Albert Popp: http://www.transpersonal.de/mbischof/englisch/webbookeng.htm
79. Body as a whole: What Doctors Don't Tell You. Sept 2015
80. Dr. Alexander Loyd, Ph.D., N.D. "The Master Key" http://www.immunesystemmasterkey.com/
81. Emotional healing: What Doctors Don't Tell You. October 2017 https://www.wddty.com/magazine/2017/october/mind-over-illness-2.html
82. Debbie Shapiro. "Your Body Speaks Your Mind!" 1996. ISBN 07499-1595-1
83. DR. Joe Dispenza "You are the Placebo: Making Your Mind Matter" ISBN: 8601404224386 (Hay House £14.99)

The Healing Code

84. Alexander Loyd, PhD, ND. Ben Johnson, MD, DO, NMD. "The Healing Code" ISBN 978-1-4555-0201-
85. Dr Bruce Lipton "The Biology of Belief – Unleashing the Power of Consciousness, Matter & Miracles" 2011. ISBN 9781848503359
86. Heart Rate Variable. (HRV) The Medical Test for Stress. https://www.ncbi.nlm.nih.gov/pmc/articles/PMC1555630/

Meditation

87. How Meditation affects your brain: https://blog.bufferapp.com/how-meditation-affects-your-brain
88. Deepak Chopra. – Free Healing Meditation. https://www.youtube.com/watch?v=IYhksvOV_vM

Music

89. Jonathan Goldman. "The 7 Secrets of Sound Healing" Revised Edition. ISBN: 9781781808290)
90. Joseph Puleo: https://www.lifeenergysolutions.com/blog/sofeggiofrequencies/
91. Michael S Tyrell. "The Healing Frequency Music Project". https://wholetones.com

EFT

92. EFT Techniques: www.theenergytherapycentre.co.uk/eft-explained.htm

Mind Management

93. The Chimp Paradox: https://joosr.com/blog/chimp-paradox-summary
94. Dr Steve Peters: Undergraduate Dean Sheffield Medical School. CEO of Chimp Management Limited.

Notes for Part 7

Air Ionisers

Further Reading

Health Benefits of Negative Air Ionizers: http://negativeionizers.net/negative-ions-benefits/
Guy Cramer : Advanced Research on Atmospheric Ions and Respiratory Problems. Sept. 2, 1996
http://mypage.direct.ca/g/gcramer/asthma.html
Scientific studies involving positive and negative ions: https://www.djclarke.co.uk/file06.html

Salt Lamps

Further Reading
Rock Salt health benefits: www.criticalcactus.com/himalayan-pink-salt-lamp-health-benefits/
Google search: Dangers of Salt Lamps. http://www.saltylamps.co.uk/aboutus.html

Near infrared Saunas
95.   Dr Lawrence Wilson: Near infrared Saunas versus Far infrared https://drlwilson.com/Articles/SAUNAS-NEAR%20VS.%20FAR%20I.htm
95.   Dr Lawrence Wilson: "Sauna Therapy" book available from Amazon.com
95.   Dr Lawrence Wilson. Far infrared Saunas: https://draxe.com/infrared-sauna/
96.   Dr William L Marcus: http://www.infraredsauna.co.uk/detoxification/
97.   Dr. Robert O. Young, cited in > Detoxification through the skin institutes, for home use and in Veterinary Medicine. https://www.zazenhealthsolutions.com/research-material/doc/1detox/doc2-iframe=true&width=850&height=500.html
98.   Dr Haller: https://trulyheal.com/hyperthermia-training/
98.   Dr Haller: https://www.nearinfraredsauna.co.uk/near-infrared-sauna
Purchasing Home Near Infrared Saunas in UK: email: contact@nearinfraredsauna.co.uk : lilahpav@yahoo.com Website: www.nearinfraredsauna.co.uk/

Hair Mineral Analysis
99.   Hair Mineral State: https://www.mineralstate.co.uk/ Email: services@mineralstate.co.ukAirnergy

Airnergy
100.   Airnergy. Obtainable from: http://www.biolifesolutions.co.uk/ Email: info@biolifesolutions.co.uk.
101.   Dr Chris Steele- TV Doctor: Spirovital Airnergy Therapy: www.airnergy-oxygen-therapy.co.uk

PolarAid Health Disc
102.   Natural Healing Energy: www.polaraidhealth.com
103.   Nikola Tesla. (July 10, 1856 to January 7, 1943) was an engineer known for designing the alternating-current (AC) electric system. He also created the "Tesla coil," which is still used in radio technology.
https://www.biography.com/people/nikola-tesla-9504443
104.   George Lakhovsky. Russian scientist believed that every cell of the human body has its own frequency. Healthy cells emit a frequency radiation. He developed the Multi Wave oscillator.
https://aurorscalartechnology.com/en/naturopathy-therapy/george-lakhovsky-and-the-multiwave-oscillator/
105.   Dr Dino Tomic. A practicing gynaecologist and obstetrician, Dr. Dino Tomic has devoted over 20 years researching alternative healing techniques. He tells us that the PolarAid is a small round flat device with no supply of electrical power, but that it achieves fantastic effects.
https://www.polaraidhealth.com/talk_with_dr_tomic/

Pulsed Electromagnetic Field Therapy Equipment EMF
106.   Manfred Fichter "Vitapulse the pulsating magnetic field" 1983
107.   Pawluk MD, MSc. Medical Authority on Magnetic Field Therapy. (www.drpawluk.com)

Resperate
108.   Dr Chris Steele: https://www.youtube.com/watch?v=t5TJPVfRIJo

Scenar
109. Soviet Space program: http://www.miamiholistic.com/links/scenar.html
110. How it Works: https://scenarworld.co.uk/scenar-how-it-works/

Zona Plus
111. Dr Ronald L Wiley. Zona Health The Power to change: https://www.zona.com/pages/science

Further Reading
Train your nervous system to control your blood pressure without drugs or supplements – https://www.youtube.com/watch?v=Hxg8j_fh0oU
https://www.zona.com/products/zona-plus-series-3
Zona Plus: https://www.zona.com

Ways to minimise Radiation sources

Earthing
112. Clinton Ober: https://www.groundology.co.uk/videos?show=benefits-of-earthing
112. Clinton Ober, Stephen T Sinatra. MD. Martin Zucker.: "Earthing-The most important health discovery ever?" ISBN 978-1-59120-283-7 http://www.groundology.co.uk/
113. Roy Riggs www.royriggs.uk

Further reading
Stephen T. Sinatra, M.D., F.A.C.C., F.A.C.N., C.N.S., C.B.T., Heart MD Institute https://heartmdinstitute.com/alternative-medicine/what-is-earthing-or-grounding/
Earthing Shoes: http://www.softstarshoes.com/earthing-shoes
Story of Grounding: https://www.youtube.com/watch?v=JpkIQGHwiEw&feature=youtu.be

Geopathic Stress
114. Jeff Jeffries: https://www.intelligentenergies.com/

WiFi
115. Roy Riggs BSc Geobiologist and EMF expert. See: www.royriggsuk also www.royriggs.co.uk

Q-Link
116. Meaningful Health: http://www.meaningfulhealthhq.com/q_link_research

Blushield
117. Active EMF Protection: www.blushield-uk.com Tel: 07913 091579

Earthcalm
118. A Whole House & Personal EMF Protection: www.earthcalm.com
119. Lloyd Burrell. "Long Term EMF Protection. Start Feeling Better Today" (E-Book) http://www.electricsense.com/
120. More Protective Systems: https://www.bioprotectivesystems.com/

Notes for Part 8

Tai Qi

Further reading
The Health Benefits of Tai Chi. December 4, 2015
https://www.health.harvard.edu/staying-healthy/the-health-benefits-of-tai-chi
The Practice of Qi Gong: http://www.taichinews.com/about-qigong
NHS Choices. 05/08/2015: https://www.nhs.uk/Livewell/fitness/Pages/taichi.aspx

The Top 10 Health Benefits of Tai Chi: By Health Fitness Revolution – March 25, 2015 http://www.healthfitnessrevolution.com/top-10-health-benefits-tai-chi/

Yoga
121.   Adam Bean. November 11, 2015. https://www.rodalesorganiclife.com/author/adam-bean
122.   "What The Doctors Don't Tell you" —WDDTY- November 2015. Support of the Digestive system:
123.   University of Maryland, School of Nursing: https://www.ncbi.nlm.nih.gov/pubmed/20105062
124.   J Altern. Complement Med. 2010 Jan 16 "The health benefits of yoga and exercise: a review of comparison studies". https://www.ncbi.nlm.nih.gov/pubmed/20105062
125.   Dana Blinder: WELLBEING YOGA. 5 Surprising Ways Yoga Affects Your Health. July 30, 2009

Pilates
126.   Joseph Hubertus Pilates (December 9, 1883–October 9, 1967). https://en.wikipedia.org/wiki/Joseph_Pilates

Further Reading
Health benefits of Pilates & Yoga: https://www.betterhealth.vic.gov.au/health/conditionsandtreatments/pilates-and-yoga-health-benefits
NHS Choices: https://www.nhs.uk/Livewell/fitness/Pages/pilates.aspx. (Reviewed 19/05/2015)

NOTES FOR PART 9

Acupuncture/Acupressure
127.   Neuroscience Letters : "Acupuncture and Endorphins". https://www.sciencedirect.com/
128.   Theory of Acupressure: https://en.wikipedia.org/wiki/Acupressure

Further reading
Healing with Acupuncture. https://yinyanghouse.com/
Janet Wright "Reflexology and Acupressure". ISBN: 9781570671494

Alexander Technique
129.   Dr. Wilfred Barlow MD. "The Alexander Principle" ISBN: 9780892813858
https://alexandertechnique.co.uk/

Further reading:
Frank Pierce Jones "Freedom to Change- Development and Science of the Alexander Technique" Paperback – 1 May 1997
Research: https://alexandertechnique.co.uk/alexander-technique/research/listing

Ayurvedic Medicine

Further reading
Ayurveda: https://en.wikipedia.org/wiki/Ayurveda
Dr. Josh Axe, DNM, DC, CNS, https://draxe.com/?s=Ayurvedic Medicine
The Chopra Center: https://chopra.com/articles/what-is-ayurveda

Bioenergetics

130. Alexander Lowen. American physician and psychotherapist who developed bioenergetic analysis: https://www.bodyflow.uk.com/bioenergetics/
131. Wilhelm Reich was an Austrian doctor of medicine and psychoanalyst, a member of the second generation of analysts after Sigmund Freud.
132. Carl Gustav Jung was a Swiss psychiatrist and psychoanalyst who founded analytical psychology.
133. Video explanation: http://devaraj.org.uk/bioenergetics/

Bioresonance/Mora Therapy

134. Dr Franz Morell & Erich Rasche: http://www.oirf.com/inst-morasuper-info.html

Further reading

Roger Coghill August 2007 Part 1
http://www.positivehealth.com/article/energy-medicine/bioresonance-fact-or-fallacy-an-evidence-based-approach
Roger Coghill August 2007 Part 2
http://www.positivehealth.com/article/energy-medicine/bioresonance-part-ii-practical-approaches-to-treatment
Dr. Volker W. Rahlfs, C. Stat. (RSS) and Dr. med. Andreas Rozehnal -Institute for Data Analysis & Study Planning Institute. https://bioresonance.com

Bowen Technique

135. Tom Bowen: http://www.bowtech.com/WebsiteProj/Pages/About/History.aspx

Chelation Therapy

136. Terry Chappell. MD. Qualified at University of Michigan 1969 Presentation of EDTA Chelation Therapy. May 15, 1993 – Dallas, Texas; November 6, 1993 – Colorado Springs, Colorado; May 6, 1993 – Houston, Texas.
137. National Institute for Health & Care Excellence (NICE): https://www.evidence.nhs.uk/search?q=Chelation+therapy
138. MD Magazine. Feb 1995 Chelation Therapy: Position Paper On EDTA Chelation Therapy American College for Advancement in Medicine (ACAM) : http://www.healthy.net/Health/Article/Position_Paper_on_EDTA_Chelation_Therapy/262
139. American College for Advancement in Medicine (ACAM) on Chelation therapy: https://www.acam.org/blogpost/1092863/ACAM-Integrative-Medicine-Blog?tag=chelation+therapy

Further reading

Life Enhancement magazine: EDTA Chelation: The Real "Miracle" Therapy for Vascular Disease
http://www.life-enhancement.com/magazine/article/78-edta-chelation-the-real-miracle-therapy-for-vascular-disease

Chiropractic & Osteopathy

140. Dr. John Bergman: https://www.drjohnbergman.com/about/
141. Explanation of McTimmony Practice: http://www.mctimoney-chiropractic-ireland.org/method.html
142. Osteopathy & NHS: https://www.nhs.uk/conditions/complementary-and-alternative-medicine/

Further reading

NHS Choices: https://www.nhs.uk/conditions/osteopathy/
NICE Assesment: https://www.evidence.nhs.uk/search?q=cranial+osteopathy

Susan Cartlidge BA, DC, MMCA : McTimoney Chiropractic: a gentle way with back pain: https://www.sciencedirect.com/science/article/pii/S1353611797800145

Robert A Leach DC. FICC. "The Chiropractic Theories. A Textbook of Scientific Research". 2004

Cheryl Hawk, Raheleh Khorsan, Anthony J. Lisi, Randy J. Ferrance, Marion Willard Evans. "A Systematic Review with Implications for Whole Systems Research". Published Online:29 Jun 2007

Epigenetics

143.   Konstantin Erikseni: https://wakeup-world.com/2012/03/26/the-science-of-epigenetics-how-our-minds-can-reprogram-our-genes/

144.   Science Direct: https://www.sciencedirect.com/topics/neuroscience/epigenetics

144.   Science Direct. Trends in Modern Medicine : https://www.sciencedirect.com/science/article/pii/S1471491409001944

145.   Bruce Lipton PhD. Author & Cellular Biologist: https://www.youtube.com/watch?v=zwOvg1rJfcM

145.   Bruce Lipton: Spontaneous Evolution: Our Positive Future And A Way To Get There From Here Paperback – 24 Feb 2011 https://www.amazon.co.uk/Spontaneous-Evolution-Positive-Future-There/dp/1848503059

Further reading:

What is Epigenetics: https://www.whatisepigenetics.com/what-is-epigenetics/
http://www.epigenetics-international.com/uploads/Handouts/Epigenetics.pdf

Homeopathy

146.   Samuel Hahnemann 1755-1843. German physician who developed Homeopathy.

147.   CAM on Homeopathy: https://homeopathycanada.com/blog

148.   CAM & Homeopathy: Spontaneous Evolution: Our Positive Future And A Way To Get There From Here Paperback – 24 Feb 2011

149.   WDDTY Feb 2016: https://www.wddty.com/news/2015/02/homeopathy-is-twice-as-effective-as-placebo.html?

150.   WDDTY May 2016: https://www.wddty.com/magazine/2016/may/the-doctors-case-for-homeopathy.html

Kinesiology

151.   What is Kinesiology? https://www.wm.edu/as/kinesiology/research/index.php

152.   Research: http://www.kinesiologyscotland.com/What-is-kinesiology-by-kinesiologist-Jim-Currie.html

Massage

153.   The Yellow Emperor's Classic of Medicine https://www.ncbi.nlm.nih.gov/pmc/articles/PMC2287209/

154.   Hippocrates: http://www.cranemassagetherapy.com/2013/01/28/hippocrates-and-massage/

Further reading

https://www.takingcharge.csh.umn.edu/explore-healing-practices/massage-therapy/what-does-research-say-about-massage-theraphy
http://www.therapyroomannan.com/nohands.html

Reflexology

Further Reading

Devaki Berkson. MA. "The Foot Book". ISBN: 0-06-463474-4

Reiki
155.   What is Reiki: http://www.reiki.org/faq/whatisreiki.html

Rolfing
156.   Dr Ida Rolf. http://www.rolfing.ch/background/

Further reading
Google Search Rolfing: http://metro.co.uk/2017/02/14/what-is-rolfing-and-do-i-need-to-be-rolfed-6251068/?ito=cbshare
Rolfing onTwitter: https://twitter.com/MetroUK | Facebook: https://www.facebook.com/MetroUK/

The Zenni Method
157.   Victor Zenni: http://www.zenniviktor.pl/nowyserwis/en/aboutviktorzenni/
158.   Zenni Method: http://revolutioninmedicine.blogspot.co.uk/2017/01/professionaland-effective-method-of.html
159.   WDDTY March 2018 Information on elimination of the cause of disease: http://www.zenniviktor.pl/nowyserwis/en/articles/files/b30ee87c3ede7fc-f4ad9d811f4f3dd36-4.html

General reading for more Alternative Therapies
(https://greatist.com/health/alternative-medicine-therapies-explained

NOTES FOR PART 10

160.   Napolean Hill: (born October 26, 1883–November 8, 1970) "Think & Grow Rich" ISBN: 009190021-29-780091-900212 (First published in the UK in 2004)
https://www.amazon.co.uk/Napoleon-Hill/e/B000APAMYE
(It must be noted that there is controversy regarding the authenticity of these claims by Napolean Hill)
161.   Winston Churchill: 1887–1965. Sir Winston Leonard Spencer-Churchill KG OM CH TD DL FRS RA was a British politician, army officer, and writer, was Prime Minister of the United Kingdom from 1940 to 1945 and again from 1951 to 1955.
https://www.goodreads.com/quotes/77097-you-create-your-own-universe-as-you-go-along
162.   Andrew Carnegie, was a Scottish-American industrialist, business magnate, and philanthropist.
163.   "The Secret" Rhonda Byrne. ISBN: 13-978-1-8473-7029
164.   Robert Kyosaki: "Rich Dad Poor Dad" ISBN 0 7515 3271 1 (Time Warner Paperback)
165.   Ralph Waldo Emerson: Born: 25 May 1803–27 April 1882. He was an American essayist, lecturer, philosopher and poet who led the transcendentalist movement of the mid-19th century. Wikipedia

Further reading
The Law of Attraction: http://applying-the-law-of-attraction.com/#ixzz5EQojAQAv
See: http://james-allen.in1woord.nl/?text=as-a-man-thinketh
Law of Abundance: https://www.briantracy.com/blog/category/personal-success/
"The Master Key" by Charles F Haanal Re printed 1977.ISBN -900604-05-0
"The Money Gym" 2010. Nicola Cairncross. ISBN 978-1-907498-01-5
"You Were Born Rich" by Bob Proctor Available from Amazon.

About the Author

Gretchen Pyves is a retired nurse midwife and health visitor. She has always been interested in health developments and keeping healthy. Having researched and acted on many theories which have stood the test of time, has led her to gather together the many ways we can take responsibility for our own health and prevent illness as far as is possible. The crisis in the NHS, being overburdened with unprecedented demands has prompted her to write this book and share her knowledge and understanding. Now 85 years she is still very active and plays veteran tennis at her club of 39 years, goes to the local gym and attends Tai Qi classes. She lives with her second husband in an 18th Century Farmhouse in Lancashire. They grow their own seasonal vegetables and fruit and keep chickens.